# THE GREEN GUIDE
# Great Britain

Grenadier Guards at Buckingham Palace, ©Peter Phipp/World Pictures/Photoshot

MICHELIN

# THEGREENGUIDE **GREAT BRITAIN**

| | |
|---|---|
| **Editorial Manager** | Jonathan P. Gilbert |
| **Principal Writer** | Paul Murphy |
| **Production Manager** | Natasha G. George |
| **Cartography** | John Dear, Josyane Rousseau, Evelyne Girard, Michèle Cana |
| **Photo Editor** | Yoshimi Kanazawa |
| **Proofreader** | Karolin Thomas |
| **Interior Design** | Chris Bell |
| **Cover Design** | Chris Bell, Christelle Le Déan |
| **Layout** | John Heath, Natasha G. George |
| **Cover Layout** | Michelin Apa Publications Ltd. |

**Contact Us**

The Green Guide
Michelin Travel and Lifestyle
One Parkway South
Greenville, SC 29615
USA
www.michelintravel.com

Michelin Travel Partner
Hannay House
39 Clarendon Road
Watford, Herts WD17 1JA   UK
☎01923 205240
www.ViaMichelin.com
travelpubsales@uk.michelin.com

**Special Sales**

For information regarding bulk sales,
customized editions and premium sales,
please contact our Customer Service
Departments:
USA      1-800-432-6277
UK        01923 205240
Canada 1-800-361-8236

# HOW TO USE THIS GUIDE

## PLANNING YOUR TRIP

The blue-tabbed PLANNING YOUR TRIP section at the front of the guide gives you **ideas for your trip** and **practical information** to help you organize it. You'll find tours, practical information, a host of outdoor activities, a calendar of events, information on shopping, sightseeing, kids' activities and more.

## INTRODUCTION

The orange-tabbed INTRODUCTION section explores Great Britain's **Nature** and geology. The **History** section spans from Roman times through Empire to the modern day. The **Art and Culture** section covers architecture, art, literature and music, while the **Country Today** delves into modern Great Britain.

## DISCOVERING

The green-tabbed DISCOVERING section features Principal Sights by region, featuring the most interesting local **Sights**, **Walking Tours**, nearby **Excursions**, and detailed **Driving Tours**. Admission prices shown are normally for a single adult.

## ADDRESSES

We've selected the best hotels, restaurants, cafes shops, nightlife and entertainment to fit all budgets. See the Legend on the cover flap for an explanation of the price categories. See the back of the guide for an index of hotels and restaurants.

### Sidebars

Throughout the guide you will find blue, orange and green-colored text boxes with lively anecdotes, detailed history and background information.

### 😊 A Bit of Advice 😊

Green advice boxes found in this guide contain practical tips and handy information relevant to your visit or to a sight in the Discovering section.

## STAR RATINGS★★★

Michelin has given star ratings for more than 100 years. If you're pressed for time, we recommend you visit the ★★★, or ★★ sights first:

| | |
|---|---|
| ★★★ | **Highly recommended** |
| ★★ | **Recommended** |
| ★ | **Interesting** |

## MAPS

😊 Places to Stay map and Principal Sights map.

😊 Maps for major cities and villages.

😊 Local tour maps.

All maps in this guide are oriented north, unless otherwise indicated by a directional arrow. The term "Local Map" refers to a map within the chapter or Tourism Region. A complete list of the maps found in the guide appears at the back of this book.

© Eric Nathan/Loop Images/Photononstop

# PLANNING YOUR TRIP

# INTRODUCTION TO GREAT BRITAIN

# DISCOVERING GREAT BRITAIN

# CONTENTS

# Welcome to Great Britain

Three unique countries and many different landscapes make up Great Britain and its surrounding isles. England, Scotland and Wales have been settled for over 700,000 years, but have only been politically unified since 1707, so it is little wonder that there are so many different cultures. Moreover, only a century or so ago, Britain ruled a quarter of the world, which has left a vast cultural legacy. In modern Britain heritage, history and high culture play a continuing role, but nothing stands still for long.

*The British Museum, London*

Y. Kanazawa/Michelin

## LONDON *(pp88–129)*

The capital is one of the most cosmo-politan, dynamic, fashionable and cultural cities on Earth, home to such quintessential images of Britain as Big Ben, Tower Bridge, red double-decker buses, and bear-skinned guards. For a crash course in British history and culture, it is an indispensable first stop.

## SURREY, KENT, SUSSEX
*(pp130–155)*

These three leafy southern counties provide the main gateways to Britain by air, rail and sea. Bohemian Brighton in summer and historic Canterbury year-round are major attractions.

## HAMPSHIRE, DORSET, WILTSHIRE *(pp156–191)*

These counties form the old heartland of Wessex, the last English kingdom to be subdued by the Danes, in the 11C. Wiltshire is world famous for Stone-henge while Dorset boasts mysteries of its own, as well as prehistoric fossils at Lyme Regis. Hampshire is home to ancient forest land and England's naval heritage. It is a rich mix where the distant past is never far away.

## CHILTERNS, OXFORDSHIRE, COTSWOLDS *(pp192–217)*

The Cotswolds are a magnet for visitors in search of idyllic English villages and rural scenery. Oxford easily justifies its reputation as one of Britain's top attractions; its university is a wealth of culture, history and architectural wonder.

## BRISTOL, BATH, SOMERSET *(pp218–237)*

Cultured Bath, with its eponymous Roman springs, and magnificent Regency architecture, is probably the finest 18C city in the world. Built upon maritime and engineering trades, buzzing Bristol has a rich dockside heritage and Georgian beauty too. Somerset boasts picturesque Cheddar Gorge and mythical Glastonbury.

## DEVON AND CORNWALL *(pp238–273)*

England's holiday playground enjoys beaches and crags, historic towns and cities, picture-postcard villages and fishing harbours, unspoiled moors and national parks, stately homes and even statelier gardens, and a fascinat-ing industrial heritage. east anglia *(p274–295)*

*Eden Project, Cornwall*

Tamsyn Williams/Eden Project

Dovedale, Peak District, Derbyshire

©Geoff Pickering/Bigstockphoto.com

Bucolic East Anglia was a favourite of Constable. Its canvas is still abundantly green, devoid of relief but full of traditional seaside resorts, preserved medieval towns and villages, extensive waterways and the beautiful university city of Cambridge.

## EAST MIDLANDS (pp296–311)

Nottingham's Robin Hood is the region's star name, and even if there is little evidence of the outlaw, the city has more than just a legend to sustain visitor interest. Lincoln Cathedral is the star attraction; Stamford is the hidden gem of this underrated region.

## WEST MIDLANDS (pp312–343)

The Industrial Revolution began here and the region's industrial heritage is unrivalled. However, unspoiled shires and countryside, magnificent country houses and great walking trails are only ever a short distance away. Shakespeare's Stratford-upon-Avon is a world-famous cultural pilgrimage.

## THE NORTHWEST (pp344–365)

The two great cities of Liverpool and Manchester dominate this area, both revived to become very visitor-friendly. The walled town of Chester is rich in Roman history, while Blackpool is the archetypal British seaside resort.

## CUMBRIA AND THE LAKES (pp366–379)

The Lake District is regarded by many visitors as England's most beautiful countryside. It has inspired poets and writers for over 200 years and is still, justifiably, one of the most popular holiday regions in Great Britain.

## YORKSHIRE (pp380–409)

Britain's largest county has more variety than any other region. The city of York, with its magnificent minster and rich Roman past, is unmissable. The great outdoors of the dales and moors beckons walkers, while more genteel tourists enjoy the towns of Harrogate and Richmond. Metro types flock to Leeds and in summer Scarborough and Whitby are seaside favourites.

## THE NORTHEAST (pp410–429)

Revitalised Newcastle-upon-Tyne is the dynamic focus of the Northeast. Nearby, the small cathedral city of Durham is one of the jewels of England. Walk in the footsteps of the Romans along Hadrian's Wall and pretend you're a wizard at Alnwick Castle.

## SCOTLAND (pp430–493)

In Scotland you'll find kilts and tartans, shortbread and whisky, bagpipes, castles and golf, alongside a modern country reinventing itself. Visit Edinburgh for its setting and history, but don't miss Glasgow for its vibrant cultural scene. Beyond lie some of the most remote parts of Britain, with breathtaking scenery, prehistory, and a way of life light years from Edinburgh's Royal Mile. Bring wet weather gear and a sense of adventure.

## WALES (pp494–521)

Like Scotland, Wales offers some of Britain's most dramatic mountain scenery and a very different historical and cultural perspective on being British. Wales is easily the least densely populated nation in Britain and across much of the Principality, four-legged creatures far outnumber people. Mighty castles, magnificent golden beaches and a fascinating industrial heritage await.

Millennium Bridge over the Thames and Tate Modern, London
© Eric Nathan/Loop Images/Photononstop

# When and Where to Go

## WHEN TO GO
### SEASONS

There is no season of the year when it's too hot, too cold, too wet or too dry for you to enjoy the sights, but the changeable British climate lives up to its reputation. Spring and autumn are the best seasons for visiting parks and gardens, when the flowers are in bloom or the leaves are turning colour; most stately homes and other country sights are closed from October to Easter. In **spring** as the days grow longer and warmer, the light is glorious, but showers are frequent. **Summer** is unpredictable with moderate temperatures; in July and August there may be occasional heat waves in the southern areas, when the thermometer tops 30°C/86°F, or the days may be cloudy and cool. **Autumn** can start dry and sunny, with clear skies and beautiful sunsets, while the air is crisp and invigorating. But as the days grow shorter, the temperature usually lowers. In **winter**, southern areas can remain fairly mild until Christmas. There may be cold snaps, but the temperature rarely drops below freezing point. However, wind and dampness can make it feel very cold. Autumn and winter are the best time for visiting museums or for shopping, as places are less crowded, except in the weeks before Christmas.

### CLIMATE

Chatting about the weather is a great British tradition, if only because it is so unpredictable and rain is seldom unaccompanied by brighter spells. The moist and breezy oceanic climate has many compensations. Stressful extremes of either heat or cold are rare, so that outdoor activity of some kind is almost always possible. Although the western mountains receive the highest amount of precipitation, which on some summits reaches an astonishing

Spring – bluebells in the woodland
© John Woodworth/iStockphoto.com

200in/5,000mm, it is in the west that the tempering effects of the **Gulf Stream** are felt and where subtropical plants can flourish in sheltered locations. The drier, sunnier climate of the east and south is more continental in character, with colder winters and warmer summers.

## WHERE TO GO
### HISTORIC PROPERTIES

Many country houses, gardens, historic monuments and ruins are owned or maintained by the following organisations, which offer free entry to their members. The **Great British Heritage Pass** (valid for 4, 7, 15 days or month, and valid for 6 months from date of purchase) gives access to over 580 properties throughout Great Britain under the care of the National Trust, English Heritage, National Trust for Scotland, Historic Scotland and Cadw. See www.britishheritagepass. com for more details. It is available from major tourist offices in the UK and may also be purchased online.

♦ **Cadw**
  **(Welsh Historic Monuments)**
  Over 125 properties: Cadw, Plas Carew, Unit 5/7 Cefn Coed, Parc Nantgarw, Cardiff CF15 7QQ, Wales.
  ℘01443 336 000.
  www.cadw.wales.gov.uk

- **English Heritage**
  Exists to protect and promote England's spectacular historic environment and ensure that its past is researched and understood. Over 400 properties: Customer Services Department, PO Box 569, Swindon SN2 2YP. ✆0870 333 1181. www.english-heritage.org.uk
- **Historic Scotland**
  An executive agency of the Scottish government, responsible for historic monuments in Scotland. Over 300 properties: Longmore House, Salisbury Place, Edinburgh EH9 1SH, Scotland. ✆0131 668 8600. www.historic-scotland.gov.uk
- **Manx National Heritage**
  National organisation for the Isle of Man responsible for eight principal sites and 4,000 acres/1,620ha: Douglas, Isle of Man, IM1 3LY. ✆01624 648 000. www.gov.im/mnh

Membership of some of the above organisations entitles discounted entry to sites owned by another.

- **National Trust**
  One of the largest landowners in the United Kingdom. Owns many heritage properties and natural beauty spots.
- **England and Wales**
  PO Box 39, Warrington WA5 7WD. ✆0844 800 1895. www.nationaltrust.org.uk
- **Scotland**
  28 Charlotte Square, Edinburgh EH2 4ET. ✆0844 493 2100. www.nts.org.uk

There are reciprocal arrangements between these trusts and similar overseas trusts.

- **The Royal Oak Foundation,**
  American public charity affiliated with the National Trust to promote the preservation of Anglo-American heritage. Royal Oak members automatically receive the rights and privileges of full National Trust (England and Wales) members.
  35 West 35th Street, Suite 1200, New York, New York 10001-2205, USA. ✆212-480-2889; 800-913-6565. www.royal-oak.org

## BEER

- **Campaign for Real Ale**
  Protects traditional draught beer and traditional pubs, organises beer festivals and produces the annual *Good Beer Guide*.
  230 Hatfield Road, St Albans, Herts AL1 4LW. ✆01727 867 201. www.camra.org.uk

## ARTS

- **British Arts Festivals Association**
  Provides advance information on leading annual arts festivals in the United Kingdom.
  2nd Floor, 28 Charing Cross Road, London WC2H 0DB. ✆020 7240 4532. www.artsfestivals.co.uk

## BATTLES

- **The Sealed Knot**
  Organises re-enactments of the battles of the English Civil War. Burlington House, Botleigh Grange Business Park, Southampton, Hampshire SO30 2DF. www.thesealedknot.org.uk

## GARDENS

Formal gardens attached to grand country houses to delightful small cottage gardens, all attest to the British passion for gardening. Plants are sometimes for sale.

- **The National Gardens Scheme**
  Publishes an annual guide – *The Yellow Book* – to private gardens that open to the public for a limited period in aid of charity. Hatchlands Park, East Clandon, Guildford, Surrey GU4 7RT. ✆01483 211 535. www.ngs.org.uk

# What to See and Do

## OUTDOOR FUN

The temperate climate of Great Britain has helped to make it the home of many outdoor sports and games. There are few days in the year when outdoor activities are impossible and the long coastline, the rivers and lakes, the mountains and lowlands provide opportunities for all kinds of sports. The mild and moist climate has fostered the development of many games played on a flat grass surface – the national pastimes being football (both "soccer" and rugby) in winter, and cricket in summer. Every weekend (weather permitting) from May to September cricket matches are played on club fields and village greens. The English Tourist Board publishes an annual guide listing contact addresses for many sports.

## CYCLING

Britain is becoming a more cycle-friendly country in spite of often heavy traffic conditions. Most local tourist information centres will give advice on cycle hire and routes, including traffic-free alternatives.

The **National Cycle Network** (www. sustrans.org.uk) comprises around 10,000 miles/16,100km of signposted cycle routes, around a third of which are traffic-free. Just click on their "Sustrans Near You" link to find routes close to where you're staying.

The national association, the Cyclists' Touring Club (CTC) can also help with itineraries and maps.

* **Cyclists' Touring Club**
  ✆0844 736 8450. www.ctc.org.uk

## HORSE RIDING

The British have a longstanding love affair with horses and there are professionally run horse-riding centres all over the country, catering to all levels, even in central London! There is no central UK organisation so ask at the nearest tourist information centre.

## GOLF

Great Britain is the spiritual home of the game and very well supplied with golf courses which range from the links courses on the coast to inland park courses. Most are privately owned but are happy to accept visitors. Municipal courses are usually very heavily used, with long queues at the first tee at weekends. In Scotland green fees are less expensive and queues are rare.

**Michelin** Maps 501 to 504 and the annual red-cover *Michelin Guide Great Britain & Ireland* give information about golf courses. For more choices visit www.uk-golfguide.com.

## GAME SHOOTING

Game shooting takes place all over Great Britain but the famous grouse moors are in Scotland and the shooting season opens on 12 August. A reputable company who organises shooting parties for groups and individuals throughout the UK is **Shooting Parties**: ✆01761 241 377. www.shootingparties.co.uk.

## SKIING

Only Scotland has ski resorts – at Lochaber, Glenshee, Lecht and Aviemore in the Cairngorms and the Nevis Range near Fort William. All have ski schools and Aviemore is the most fully developed resort. Forest trails have been opened up for cross-country skiing. The best snow conditions are usually found in March and April but up-to-the minute snow reports are essential. Information available from **Ski Scotland;** http://ski.visit scotland.com. There are several dry ski slopes all over Great Britain.

## HIKING AND CLIMBING

Throughout the country there are many miles of bridleways and official footpaths, including way marked **Long Distance Footpaths** which give access to some of the best hill and coastal scenery. Some of the best walking and hiking is provided by the national parks. For fell-walkers and mountaineers, the Lake District, Wales and Scotland provide the most challenging ascents. All hikers and climbers should be aware of potential dangers and be properly equipped. Climbers are also advised to inform the police, or someone responsible, of their plans before hazardous climbs.

♦ **Ramblers Association**
www.ramblers.org.uk;
www.getwalking.org
♦ **British Mountaineering Council**
www.thebmc.co.uk

## ON THE WATER

Britain has many miles of coastline, estuaries, rivers, lakes and canals, all of which offer facilities for enjoying the water.

### Boating, Sailing and Cruising

There are all kinds of opportunities for amateur and professional sailors – a cabin cruiser on the Norfolk Broads, a narrowboat on the canal network, a punt or a rowing boat on the river. On the rivers, lakes and reservoirs there are marinas and moorings for cruisers, yachts and sailing boats; along the coast there are facilities for ocean-going yachts.

Most of the **canal network** has been rescued from dereliction, to offer angling, pleasant towpath walks and cruises and holidays on narrowboats.

♦ **Norfolk Broads**
www.enjoythebroads.com
♦ **British Waterways**
www.waterscape.com

### Windsurfing and Waterskiing

Schools and changing facilities for windsurfers are available on many inland waters and at popular places along the coast. Newquay is the UK's surfing capital and the English Surf School is the best source of information; try also www.surfing-waves.com. If you wish to waterski or wakeboard, some clubs offer a day membership system.

♦ **English Surf School**
www.englishsurfschool.com

*Narrowboat on the River Avon*

©Ann Taylor-Hughes/iStockphoto.com

♦ **British Water Ski & Wakeboard**
www.britishwaterski.org.uk

## FISHING

There are over 3.7 million fishermen in Britain. The season for coarse fishing/angling (which applies to freshwater fish, other than trout, salmon and char) runs from 15 March to 15 June; permits and advice on local waters can be obtained from any tackle shop. The waters around Britain provide ample opportunity for anglers to test their skills. Salmon and trout fishing, for which licences are required, is found in Scotland, England and Wales. Sea-angling is popular, particularly along the southwestern and Northumbrian coastlines. Sea angling festivals are regular features in some resorts.

♦ **Angling Trust**
www.anglingtrust.net
♦ **Salmon and Trout Association**
www.fishpal.com/
SalmonAndTrout

## NATURAL BRITAIN

The 15 national parks in England, Wales and Scotland are areas of protected natural beauty set aside for conservation and recreation. In addition to marked trails there are picnic sites, visitor centres and facilities for outdoor activities. For full

*Fishing on Loch Awe, Kilchurn Castle in the background, Argyll and Bute, Scotland*

© P. Tomkins/VisitScotland/Scottish Viewpoint

details, visit www.nationalparks.gov.uk and for more details of all the parks in this guide, ⓘ *see the Discovering Section*. On a smaller, local level are **National Nature Reserves** (NNRs). These include wildfowl sanctuaries, sand dunes, moorland and a variety of other ecological areas.

For details, visit www.naturalengland.org.uk or (for Scotland) www.nnr-scotland.org.uk, and www.snh.org.uk.

The following are Britain's leading animal conservation organisations:
- **Royal Society for the Protection of Birds**
  www.rspb.org.uk
- **Wildfowl and Wetlands Trust**
  www.wwt.org.uk
- **Scottish Wildlife Trust**
  www.swt.org.uk

## ACTIVITIES FOR KIDS

In this guide, sights of *particular* interest to children are indicated with a KIDS symbol (👫), though rare these days is the visitor attraction that does not cater in some way for young ones. All attractions offer discount fees for children and the vast majority also offer discounted family tickets for two or more children.

## SHOPPING
### OPENING HOURS

Traditional British shopping hours are Mondays to Saturdays from 9am/9.30am to 5.30pm/6pm. Many larger shops, particularly in out-of-town locations, also open Sundays from 10am or 11am to 4pm. There is late-night shopping (until 7pm/8pm) in most large cities on Wednesdays or Thursdays; supermarkets usually close later than other shops. Smaller individual shops may close during the lunch hour; on the other hand some stay open until very late. Many towns have an early closing day when shops are closed during the afternoon. Traditionally the winter sales before and after Christmas and New Year, and the summer sales in June and July have always been a popular time for shopping, as prices are reduced on a great range of goods. However, sales now appear on the High Street at other times of year too.

### WHAT TO BUY

Britain is one of the great shop windows of the world, famed in so many spheres of production.
For many visitors clothing is top of the shopping list. There is a huge choice of woollen articles in cashmere or lambswool, particularly in Scotland; classic styles are sold by well-known names such as Jaeger, Burberry, Marks

and Spencer, John Lewis, Debenhams and House of Fraser. The very best made-to-measure (bespoke) clothing for men is traditionally available in London in Savile Row (tailors) and Jermyn Street (shirt-makers), though these days many of the larger provincial cities (Birmingham, Manchester, Leeds, and of course the capitals of Edinburgh and Cardiff) boast outlets that are equally fashionable. The best makes of traditional porcelain – Wedgwood, Royal Worcester, Royal Doulton – are available in London and elsewhere while very acceptable "seconds" can be bought at the factory or in "reject shops". Great Britain is equally well known for its modern wares.
Antique shops and markets abound in Britain and although it is becoming increasingly difficult to find bargains in mainstream outlets, lovers of historical bric-a-brac and smaller, less valuable items will find plenty to divert them. Popular foodie souvenirs include Scotch whisky, smoked salmon, tea and marmalade.

## BOOKS
### Reference/Biography
*A Brief History of British Kings & Queens - Mike Ashley (2002).* A useful and interesting biography of all the country's rulers.

### Travel
*Notes from a Small Island - Bill Bryson (1995: 2001).* Amusing account of Bryson's first trip to Britain and its many foibles.

### Fiction
*Brighton Rock - Graham Greene (1938).* Violence and gang war are the themes of this murder thriller set in the 1930s in the famous seaside resort of Brighton.
*England England - Julian Barnes (2000).* A satire on the country's obsession with heritage featuring a "theme park England" on the Isle of Wight.
*Fever Pitch - Nick Hornby (1992).* Hornby specialises in the modern British male, in this case, an autobiographical obsession with football and specifically Arsenal Football Club. Also see: *High Fidelity* by Nick Hrnby.
*Oliver Twist - Charles Dickens (1838).* Dickens' most famous work is a strident social commentary on a grim and unforgiving London, albeit with a happy ending for Oliver, if not for all. Also see: *Great Expectations, David Copperfield, Our Mutual Friend.*
*Tess of the D'Urbervilles - Thomas Hardy (1891).* This tragedy of class consciousness and sexual double standards paints an indelible picture of England's fading rural West Country. Also see: *Far from the Madding Crowd* by Thomas Hardy.
*The Buddha of Suburbia - Hanif Kureishi (1990).* A darkly comic romp through the lives, hopes and fears of young Asians in the London of the 1980s.

## RECENT FILMS
*Four Weddings and a Funeral (1994).* A romantic comedy drama set in the 1990s following the lives and loves of a group of friends set around the title events.
*Trainspotting (1996).* The mean (non-tourist) streets of Edinburgh is the setting for this disturbing story about disaffected youths turning to heroin.
*The Full Monty (1997).* Six unemployed steel workers from Sheffield form an unlikely male striptease act in this comedy drama set in the post-industrial North of England.
*Billy Elliot (1999).* An inspiring and sometimes gritty tale set in a northern England mining town during the Miners Strikes of 1984 where a young boy discovers his talent for ballet.
*Calendar Girls (2003).* Based on a true story, a group of mature Women's Institute ladies in North Yorkshire decide to raise funds for charity by posing nude

for a calendar and in the process become internationally famous.

*Pride and Prejudice* (2005). Beautiful costume drama adaptation of the Jane Austen novel, set in an idyllic Georgian England.

*The Queen* (2006). Concerning the intriguing interaction between Queen Elizabeth II and Prime Minister Tony Blair following the death of Diana, Princess of Wales in 1997.

*Atonement* (2007). A 13-year-old irrevocably changes the course of several lives when she accuses her older sister's lover of a crime he did not commit in this haunting romantic drama. Beautifully shot, very atmospheric.

*This Is England* (2008). Racism, xenophobia. and class warfare via the violent teen movements of the early-1980s. Not for the fainthearted.

*An Education* (2009). This tender coming-of-age story about a teenage girl evokes the spirit of 1960s London and the suburbs.

*The King's Speech* (2010). The unlikely true tale of the fascinating relationship between King George VI and his unorthodox speech therapist.

# Calendar of Events

**25 JANUARY**

**Scotland** – Burns Night: a celebration of the Scottish poet, Robert Burns, featuring a supper of haggis and whisky. www.scotland.org

**LAST TUESDAY IN JANUARY**

**Lerwick, Shetland** – Up Helly Aa: torchlit procession, burning of Viking longship, night-long celebrations. www.up-helly-aa.org.uk

**APRIL**

**Putney** – Oxford–Cambridge Boat Race. www.theboatrace.org

**LATE APRIL–EARLY MAY**

**Spalding** – Flower Parade and Festival. www.spaldingnet.com

**Helston** – Flora Day Furry Dance: spectacular processional dances throughout May Day (1 May).

**MAY**

**London** – Chelsea Flower Show. www.rhs.org.uk/chelsea

**MAY–AUGUST**

**Glyndebourne** – Festival of Music and Opera. www.glyndebourne.com

**MAY–OCTOBER**

**Pitlochry** – Pitlochry Festival Theatre Season. www.pitlochry.org.uk

**EARLY MAY–MID-SEPTEMBER**

**Peak District** – Well Dressing: in such Peak villages as Eyam, Monyash, Warksworth and Youlgreave. www.derbyshireuk.net

**LATE MAY–EARLY JUNE**

**Isle of Man TT** – motor cycle races. www.iomtt.com

**LAST WEEKEND IN MAY**

**Blair Castle** – Atholl Highlanders Annual Parade, Highland Games. www.blair-castle.co.uk

**JUNE**

**Ascot** – Royal Ascot (the highlight of the British horse-racing calendar). www.ascot.co.uk

**Aldeburgh Festival**: classical music festival. www.aldeburgh.co.uk

**2ND OR 3RD SATURDAY IN JUNE**

**London** – Trooping the Colour: the Queen's official birthday parade on Horse Guards Parade. www.army.mod.uk/events

*Edinburgh Military Tattoo*

P. Tomkins/VisitScotland/Scottish Viewpoint

### LATE JUNE–EARLY JULY
**Wimbledon** – Lawn Tennis Championships. www.wimbledon.com

**Ludlow** – Shakespeare Festival. www.ludlowfestival.co.uk

**Henley Royal Regatta**: premier amateur regatta. www.hrr.co.uk

### 2ND WEEK IN JULY
**Llangollen** – International Eisteddfod. International Musical Competitions. www.llangollen.com

### MID–LATE JULY
**King's Lynn** – Festival of Music (Classical and Jazz) and the Arts. www.kingslynnfestival.org.uk

### MID–JULY–SEPTEMBER
**London** – Henry Wood Promenade Concerts (BBC Proms): Royal Albert Hall. www.royalalberthall.com

### 3RD WEEK IN JLUY
**River Thames** – Swan-Upping: marking of swans on the Thames. www.royalswan.co.uk

### AUGUST
**Jersey** – Battle of Flowers: floral- inspired carnival. www.battleofflowers.com

**Aboyne** – Highland Games. www.aboynegames.com

**Edinburgh** – Edinburgh International Festival, including the Military Tattoo and the Fringe. www.eif.co.uk

**Oban** – Argyllshire Highland Gathering. www.obangames.com

**London** – Notting Hill Carnival. www.nottinghill-carnival.co.uk

### SEPTEMBER–OCTOBER
**Blackpool** – Blackpool Illuminations. www.blackpooltourism.com

### 1ST SATURDAY IN SEPTEMBER
**Braemar** – Highland Gathering. www.braemargathering.org

### 1ST SUNDAY IN NOVEMBER
**London to Brighton** – Veteran Car Run. www.lbvcr.com

### 5 NOVEMBER
**Throughout the country** – fireworks and bonfires commemorate Guy Fawkes and the Gunpowder Plot.

*Notting Hill Carnival, London.*

© Jon Arnold/hemis.fr

### Summer Music Festivals

Britain is well served with music festivals. The biggest is Glastonbury. Other festivals that attract big name acts are Reading Festival; Leeds Festival; O2 Wireless Festival, Hyde Park, London; V Festival, Weston Park, Staffs; Isle of Wight Festival. Popular crossover music and world music festivals include Bestival (Isle of Wight) and WOMAD (Charlton Park, Wilts). Visit www.efestivals.co.uk.

**2ND SATURDAY IN NOVEMBER**
**London** – Lord Mayor's Show and Procession. www.lordmayorsshow.org

**LATE NOVEMBER–
EARLY DECEMBER**
**London** – State Opening of Parliament. www.parliament.uk

**DECEMBER**
**London** – Christmas highlights in London include Midnight Mass at St Paul's Cathedral; lights and dressed shop windows on Regent Street (*www.regent streetonline.com*) and Oxford Street (www.oxfordstreet.co.uk); and the enormous Trafalgar Square Christmas tree.
**Edinburgh** – On New Year's Eve Scots celebrate "Hogmanay" in riotous fashion (throughout the country).

# Know Before You Go

## USEFUL WEBSITES
### VISIT BRITAIN

The website of **Visit Britain**, the country's official tourist authority, is www.visit.britain.com. However, the official national websites are more user-friendly.
All offer accommodation, holidays, what to see and do, links to all geographical areas and subsections on sports and culture:
  ♦ **www.visitengland.com**
  ♦ **www.visitscotland.com**
  ♦ **www.visitwales.com**

The official website for **London**:
  ♦ **www.visitlondon.com**

The official website for **Edinburgh**:
  ♦ **www.edinburgh.org**

## OTHER WEBSITES
### London
  ♦ **www.londontown.com**
  ♦ **www.timeout.com/london**

### Travel Planning
  ♦ **www.viamichelin.com**
    Plan your trip with Michelin's online route planner via the best places to see, dine and stay. Explore further with Michelin's online magazines for tourists, motorists and gastronomists. You can even upload details of your own journeys and discover other users' favourite journeys to download onto your Michelin GPS.

### Scotland and Wales
  ♦ **www.scotland-info.co.uk**
    The 80,000-word Guide to Scotland is a personal labour of love by a Scottish author, largely based on her personal travels. A very professional site with excellent suggestions on accommodation.
  ♦ **www.aboutscotland.com**
    Well-designed good looking site, with clickable maps, good pictures, personally tested accommodation and lively features and articles about visiting Scotland.

◆ **www.walesinfo.com**
Entertaining and attractive
visitors website with personal
recommendations.

### News
◆ **www.bbc.co.uk/news**
The BBC front page with breaking
news, magazine stories and links
to the rest of the **BBC website**.

## TOURIST OFFICES
**Visit Britain**, formerly known as the
British Tourist Authority provides
assistance in planning a trip to Great
Britain and an excellent range of
brochures and maps.

It works in cooperation with the three
National Tourist Boards (for England,
Wales and Scotland), the Regional
Tourist Boards and other tourist
organisations.

The **British Travel Centre** is
located at 1 Lower Regent Street,
London SW1Y 4NS: ℘0870 156 6366
(infoline).

There are **tourist information
centres** in all parts of the country
with information on sightseeing,
accommodation, places to eat,
transport, entertainment, sports
and local events. They are usually
well signposted, but some are open
only during the summer season; the
address and telephone number of
the local tourist office can be found in
sidebars throughout this guide.

Visit Britain has over 40 offices
worldwide including Belgium, Brazil,
Denmark, Germany, Hong Kong,
Ireland, Italy, Japan, the Netherlands,
Norway, Spain, Sweden and
Switzerland as well as those listed
on the opposite page.

## INTERNATIONAL VISITORS
**EMBASSIES AND CONSULATES**
### Australia
◆ **High Commission:**
Australia House, The Strand,
London WC2B 4LA.
℘020 7379 4334.
www.uk.embassy.gov.au

◆ **Honorary Consulate Scotland:**
Mr Richard Jeffrey,
Chamber of Commerce,
Capital House, 2 Festival Square,
Edinburgh EH3 9SU.
℘0131 538 0852.

### Canada
◆ **High Commission & Consulate:**
Canada House, Trafalgar
Square, London SW1Y 5BJ
(closed until summer 2012).
Temporary headquarters:
Macdonald House,
1 Grosvenor Square,
London W1K 4AB.
℘020 7258 6600.
www.canada.org.uk

### Japan
◆ **Embassy and Consulate:**
101 Piccadilly, London W1J 7JT.
℘020 7465 6500.
www.uk.emb-japan.go.jp
◆ **Consulate Scotland:**
2 Melville Crescent, Edinburgh
EH3 7HW. ℘0131 225 4777.
www. edinburgh.uk.emb-
japan.go.jp

### New Zealand
◆ **High Commission:**
New Zealand House,
80 Haymarket, London SW1Y 4TQ.
℘020 7930 8422.
www.nzembassy.com
◆ **Honorary Consulate, Scotland:**
℘0131 222 8109.

### South Africa
◆ **High Commission:**
South Africa House, Trafalgar
Square, London WC2N 5DP.
℘020 7451 7299.
http://southafricahouseuk.com

### USA
◆ **Embassy:**
24–31 Grosvenor Square, London
W1A 1AE. ℘020 7499 9000.
www.usembassy.org.uk.
Note: the US Embassy will
be relocating to Nine Elms,
Wandsworth. Call the Information

**BRITISH TOURIST AUTHORITY OFFICES (ALL OFFICES: WWW.VISITBRITAIN.COM)**

| United States | 551 5th Avenue, Suite 701, New York, NY 1017. ☎212-986-1188 |
| | 625 North Michigan Avenue, Suite 1001, IL 60611, Chicago. ☎312-787-0464 |
| | 10880 Wilshire Boulevard, Suite 570, CA 90024, Los Angeles. ☎310 470 2782 |
| Canada | 5915 Airport Road, Suite 120, Mississauga, L4V 1T1, Ontario. ☎905-405-1720 |
| France | 22 Avenue Franklin Roosevelt, 75008, Paris. ☎01 58 36 50 50 |
| Australia | Level 2, 15 Blue Street, North Sydney, NSW 2060. ☎2 90 21 44 00 |
| New Zealand | 17th Floor, 151 Queen Street, Auckland 1. ☎09 309 1899 |

Resource Center between 10am and noon, Mon–Fri. ☎020 7894 0925 for date of move.

♦ **Consulate Scotland:**
3 Regent Terrace, Edinburgh EH7 5BW. ☎0131 556 8315 (emergency only).
http://edinburgh.usconsulate.gov

♦ **Welsh Affairs Office:**
☎020 7984 0131.
http://cardiff.usvpp.gov

## ENTRY REQUIREMENTS

EU nationals should hold some means of identification, such as a **passport**. Non-EU nationals must be in possession of a valid national passport. Loss or theft should be reported to the appropriate embassy or consulate and to the local police. A visa to visit the United Kingdom is not required by nationals of the member states of the European Union and of the Commonwealth (including Australia, Canada, New Zealand and South Africa) and the USA. Nationals of other countries should check with the British Embassy and apply for a visa if necessary in good time.

The US Department of State provides useful information for US nationals on obtaining a passport, visa requirements, customs regulations, medical care, etc. for international travel online at http://travel.state.gov.

## CUSTOMS

Tax-free allowances for various commodities are governed by EU legislation except in the Channel Islands and the Isle of Man, which have different regulations. Details of these allowances and restrictions are available at most ports of entry to Great Britain.

It is prohibited to import into the United Kingdom any drugs, firearms and ammunition, obscene material featuring children, counterfeit merchandise, unlicensed livestock (birds or animals), anything related to endangered species (furs, ivory, horn, leather) and certain plants (potatoes, bulbs, seeds, trees).

British customs regulations and "duty free" allowances are outlined on their website; visit www.hmrc.gov.uk (insert Customs Allowances in 'Search').

US allowances can be found at http://travel.state.gov.

## HEALTH

Visitors to Britain are entitled to treatment at the Accident and Emergency Departments of National Health Service hospitals. For an overnight or longer stay in hospital, payment will probably be required. It is therefore advisable to take out adequate insurance cover before leaving home. Visitors from EU countries should apply to their own National Social Security Offices for a **European Health Insurance Card** (EHIC) – the replacement for Form E111 – which entitles them to medical treatment under an EU Reciprocal Medical Treatment arrangement. Nationals of non-EU countries should take out comprehensive insurance. American Express offers a service, "Global Assist", for any medical, legal or personal emergency – visit www.americanexpress.com (from outside the USA you can call collect ☎715-343-7977).

## ACCESSIBILITY

Many of the sights described in this guide are accessible to disabled people; they are designated by the ♿ symbol in the Entry Times and Charges for the attractions. However, this symbol should not be taken to signify anything other than general accessibility (as specified by the attraction) and it is always advisable to call ahead.
The red-cover **Michelin Guide Great Britain & Ireland** indicates hotels with facilities suitable for disabled people; it is advisable to book in advance. The **Royal Association for Disability and Rehabilitation** (RADAR) publishes an annual guide *Open Britain*, as well as *Accessible Scotland*, with information on hotels and holiday centres as well as sections on transport, accommodation for children and activity holidays. Call RADAR, ✆ 020 7250 3222, or shop online, www.radar-shop.org.uk. A useful government website is www.direct.gov.uk/en/Disabled People/TravelHolidaysAndBreaks, which gives information on tailored holidays and breaks for disabled people, families and carers. Other organisations such as Visit Britain, the National Trust and the Department of Transport publish info booklets.
**Tourism For All** is the national charity for UK residents: ✆ 0845 124 9971. **www.tourismforall.org.uk**.

# Getting There and Getting Around

## BY AIR

Various national and other independent airlines operate services to the capital's five airports. Heathrow and Gatwick service the majority of flights:

- **Heathrow (LHR)**
- **Gatwick (LGW)**
- **Luton (LTN)**
- **Stansted (STN)**
- **City (LCY)**

Services also run to major regional airports (Aberdeen, Birmingham, Cardiff, Edinburgh, Glasgow, Liverpool, Manchester, Newcastle, Prestwick).

## BY SEA

There are numerous cross-Channel (passenger and car ferries, hovercraft) and other ferry or shipping services from the continent. For details apply to travel agencies or to the ferry companies.

- **Brittany Ferries**
  ✆ 0818 300 400.
  www.brittanyferries.com

- **Irish Ferries**
  ✆ (353) 818 300 400.
  www.irishferries.com
- **P&O Ferries**
  ✆ 08716 642 121.
  www.poferries.com
- **Stena Line**
  ✆ 08705 70 70 70.
  www.stenaline.com

## BY TRAIN

The **Channel Tunnel** provides a direct Eurostar rail link from London St Pancras International to France and Belgium. Eurostar also runs from Ebbsfleet International and from Ashford International station (both in Kent). There is also a road/rail link between Folkestone and Calais (France).

- **Eurostar**
  www.eurostar.com
  ✆ 08432 186 186
  (ticket and bookings);
  ✆ 01777 77 78 79
  (international customer relations).

**BritRail and InterRail Passes** are available to overseas visitors and are well worth considering if you intend to travel extensively in Britain by rail, particularly given the relatively high cost of rail travel if you buy tickets while in Britain. (Note that Eurail passes are *not* valid for train travel in Great Britain.)European residents (including Brits) can use the InterRail Pass, but you can only buy a BritRail Pass if you are not a UK resident. BritRail Passes allow travel on consecutive days for various periods. These concessions can be obtained only outside Britain and should be purchased from appointed agents before the beginning of the journey in question. For more details on BritRail passes, visit www.britrail.com; for details of InterRail passes visit www.raileurope.co.uk.

Once you are in Great Britain, for information on rail services and on other concessionary tickets, including combined train and bus tickets, call ☎08457 48 49 50. www.nationalrail. co.uk. To buy train tickets, either go to the station, or buy online in advance at www.thetrainline.com or from the individual train operators.

## BY COACH/BUS

National Express, in association with other bus operators, runs express coach services covering the whole country.
☎0875 808 080 (national call centre). www.nationalexpress.com.
Cheap intercity bus companies include www.megabus.co.uk while www.easybus.co.uk offers cheap airport transfer services to and from central London.
For comprehensive public transport information in the UK, call ☎0871 200 22 33 or visit www.traveline.org.uk.

## BY CAR
### DOCUMENTS

EU nationals require a valid **national driving licence**; US nationals require a driving licence valid for 12 months – a permit is available from your local branch of the American Automobile Association: ☎www.aaa.com.
Other nationals require an international driving licence.
If you intend bringing your own

vehicle to the UK, you will need to have the **registration papers** (log-book) for the vehicle and a nationality plate of the approved size.

## INSURANCE

Insurance cover is compulsory and although an **International Insurance Certificate** (Green Card) is no longer a legal requirement in Britain, it is the most effective proof of insurance cover and is internationally recognised by the police and other authorities.
Certain UK motoring organisations offer accident insurance and breakdown service plans for members. Europ-Assistance (*www.europ-assist ance.co.uk*) and the American Automobile Association (*www.aaa. com*) have special plans for their respective memberships.

## MOTORING ORGANISATIONS

The major motoring organisations in Great Britain are the Automobile Association and the Royal Automobile Club. Each provides services in varying degrees for non-resident members of affiliated clubs.
**Automobile Association**
☎0800 085 2721
(breakdown cover sales).
**www.theaa.com**

**Royal Automobile Club**
☎0800 197 7815 (breakdown cover). **www.rac.co.uk**

## ROAD REGULATIONS

The **minimum driving age** is 17 years old. Traffic drives **on the left** and overtakes on the right. Headlights must be used at night even in built-up areas and at other times when visibility is poor.
There are severe penalties for driving after drinking more than the legal limit of alcohol.
Important traffic signs are shown at the end of the red-cover *Michelin Guide Great Britain & Ireland*.
Signage in the UK corresponds in general to international norms.

### Congestion Charging

At present London is the only city, in the UK with a congestion charge. This is payable by drivers entering the central part of the city Mon–Fri 7am–6pm. Driving into London is not recommended for visitors at any time, but if you do have to bring in your vehicle at these times, then you must familiarise yourself with how to pay by visiting www.tfl.gov.uk/roadusers/congestioncharging.

©Transport for London 2005

### Seat Belts

It is compulsory for all passengers to wear seat belts in the UK.

### Speed Limits

**Maximum speeds are:**

- **70mph/112kph**, motorways or dual carriageways
- **60mph/96kph**, other roads
- **30mph/48kph**, in towns and cities.

## PARKING

Off-street parking is indicated by blue signs with white lettering (Parking or P); payment is made on leaving or in advance for a certain period. There are also parking meters, disc systems and paying parking zones; in the last case tickets must be obtained from ticket machines (small change necessary) and displayed inside the windscreen. Illegal parking is liable to fines and also in certain cases to the vehicle being clamped or towed away. The usual restrictions are as follows:

- **Double red line** = no stopping at any time (freeway)
- **Double yellow line** = no parking at any time
- **Single yellow line** = no parking for set periods as indicated on panel
- **Dotted yellow line** = parking limited to certain times only.

## ROUTE PLANNING

The whole of Great Britain is covered by the **Michelin map series 501-504** (scale 1:400,00) and the **Michelin Road Atlas of Great Britain and Ireland** (scale 1: 300,000). In addition to the usual detailed road information, they indicate tourist features such as beaches or bathing areas, swimming pools, golf courses, racecourses, scenic routes, tourist sights, country parks, etc. These publications are an essential complement to the annual **Michelin Guide Great Britain & Ireland**, which offers an up-to-date selection of hotels and restaurants organised alphabetically by town, all inspected and graded by Michelin and marked on maps throughout.

Traffic in and around towns is heavy during the rush hour (morning and evening). It is also very heavy on major roads at the weekend in summer, particularly bank holiday weekends.

## CAR RENTAL

There are car rental agencies at airports, railway stations and in all large towns throughout Great Britain. European cars usually have manual transmission but automatic cars are available on demand. An international driving licence is required for non-EU nationals. Most companies will not rent to drivers aged under 21 or 25. The following firms operate on a national basis:

- **Avis**
  ℘0844 581 0147.
  www.avis.co.uk
- **Budget**
  ℘0844 544 3470.
  www.budget.co.uk
- **National Car Rental**
  ℘0871 3840 1140
  www.nationalcar.co.uk

- **EasyCar**
  www.easycar.com. No telephone bookings.
- **Europcar**
  ✆0871 384 9847.
  www.europcar.co.uk.
- **Hertz**
  ✆0870 844 8844.
  www.hertz.co.uk

## PETROL/GAS

In service stations dual-pumps are the rule. Unleaded pumps have green handles or a green stripe.

## TOLLS

Tolls are rare; they are levied only on the most recent bridges (London QE II, Severn, Humber and Skye), the M6 toll road (bypasses Birmingham traffic), a few minor country bridges as well as road tunnels (Dartford, Tyne).

## DRIVING CONDITIONS

In general, the closer you are to London and the Southeast, the more congested the roads become. If you intend making a major city (particularly London) the base for your trip, don't consider driving at all. In this case, using public transport for any excursions out of town is a much better idea than car hire.

All major (and many minor) cities and towns in Britain suffer traffic problems and you should avoid rush hours (7.30am to 9.30am and 5pm to 6.30pm) wherever possible.

# Where to Stay and Eat

✕ *Hotel and restaurant listings can be found in the Address Books featured throughout the guide.*

## WHERE TO STAY
## USEFUL WEBSITES
### www.visitbritain.com

The official Visit Britain site includes Britain's largest accommodation listing with over 37,000 places to stay.

### www.viamichelin.com

Plan your trip around some of Britain's finest places to see, dine and stay with Michelin's online route planner and magazine.

### www.distinctlydifferent.co.uk

Visit this site if you would like to stay in a former windmill, a lighthouse, a church, a gypsy caravan, dovecote…

## TYPES OF ACCOMMODATION

Accommodation in Britain runs the whole range, from a room in a characterful historic pub to an anonymous but (usually) comfortable night in a chain hotel, from a cheap room in a B&B (bed and breakfast in a private house) to being pampered in some of the world's finest and most sophisticated hotels. Though these days even some B&Bs have gone "designer-boutique" and can cost more than a conventional hotel room with more facilities.

London is still the most expensive place to stay in the UK, though some top hotel rates in the big provincial cities are now on a par with London prices. If price is not a problem, you can find top-quality designer hotels, many offering spa facilities and wellness treatments, in many large British cities and all over the countryside.

At the other end of the price spectrum, there is also a proliferation of no-frills chain hotels offering very competitive deals.

Wherever you choose to stay, try to book in advance online for the best deals, but if you do simply turn up at the hotel desk, ask what is the best deal they can offer you (do not simply accept the published room rate) and be prepared to haggle – the later in the day it is, the better your chances of securing a cheaper room.

## RESERVATION SERVICES

Most tourist information centres will provide, free of charge, an information booklet listing all hotels, bed-and-breakfast and other accommodation. Many will arrange accommodation for a small fee. Room prices are normally just that – the price per room – however, even for a double room, they may be quoted per person. In London the **British Hotels Reservation Centre** can help. They have 14 outlets located at London airports and main railway stations. ✆020 7592 3055. www.bhronline.com.

## BUDGET ACCOMMODATION

### Bed and Breakfast (B&B)

Many private individuals take in a limited number of guests. Prices include bed and breakfast, usually the cooked variety. A few offer an evening meal though the choice will of course be limited. Local tourist information centres usually have a list of the bed-and-breakfast establishments in the area and book if necessary for a fee. Many houses advertise with a "B&B" sign.

♦ **Put Me Up**
✆01223 852 920.
www.putmeup.co.uk

### Rural Accommodation

An interesting way of spending a holiday is to stay on one of the many different types of working farm – arable, livestock, hill or mixed – sometimes set in the heart of glorious countryside. For information apply for the booklet **Farm Stay UK** supplied by the company of the same name: ✆024 7669 6909. www.farmstayuk.co.uk.

### Universities and Colleges

During summer holidays many universities and colleges offer low-cost accommodation in the halls of residence for as little as £30 a night. ✆0114 249 3090. www.venuemasters.co.uk.

### Youth Hostels

The 250 youth hostels in Great Britain are open to members of the **Youth Hostel Association**, or to those with an international membership card. ✆0800 0191 700 (reservations). www.yha.org.uk.

♦ **Scottish Youth Hostel Association**
✆01786 891 400 (general enquiries); 0845 293 7373 (reservations). www.syha.org.uk

♦ **International Youth Hostel Federation**
✆01707 324 170. www.hihostels.com

### Camping

Visit Britain publishes **Camping and Caravanning in Britain** and local tourist information centres supply lists of camping and caravan sites.

♦ The **Camping and Caravanning Club**
✆0845 130 7632. www.campingand caravanningclub.co.uk

## WHERE TO EAT
## USEFUL WEBSITES

### www.viamichelin.com

A useful trip planner featuring some of Britain's finest places to stay and eat alongside a gastronomy, tourism and motoring magazine.

### www.squaremeal.co.uk

Reviews of restaurants and bars in London and around the UK by food critics, alongside foodie event reviews.

### www.london-eating.co.uk

This site is based on reader reviews and also features money-saving offers.

## RESTAURANTS

Dining out in the UK has undergone a revolution in the last two decades and now ranks among the very best in the world. Thanks to its colonial past and its cosmopolitan nature, the UK offers authentic tastes from all over the world, often cooked by native chefs, or collected, magpie-like, by celebrity chefs from culinary tours of the world. Restaurants are becoming less and less formal with only the top hotel dining rooms and traditional establishments still stipulating dress codes. Hours too have become more flexible though many places still serve lunch from around 12 noon to around 2.30pm and dinner from around 7pm to 10pm, and close in between. Only in London and the more buzzing metropolises will you find a good selection of late-dining restaurants. Prices tend to be high compared to many other parts of the world, though eating at lunchtime from set menus can save you a small fortune.

Making a reservation for weekend nights and Sunday lunchtime is recommended and if you want to eat in Britain's top restaurants you may need to book weeks in advance (though it's always worth checking at the last minute for cancellations). A selection of places to eat can be found in the Address Books throughout this guide. The Legend at the back of the book explains the symbols used in the Address Books.

## BISTROS, BRASSERIES AND CAFÉS

These European-style establishments, usually serving a variety of relatively simple, pan-European dishes, are the places for snacks, informal meals and drinks in trendy upbeat surroundings right throughout the day and night. The UK now has a profusion of US-style cafés, (most notably Starbucks) on the high streets of most large towns. Less common these days is the traditional English café, sometimes called a "caff' or "greasy spoon".

This is traditionally the place for a good old-fashioned fry-up (bacon, eggs, sausages, etc.), washed down with a mug of strong tea.

## PUBS (PUBLIC HOUSES)

### Gastropubs

Eating out in public houses ("pubs") has changed enormously over the last decade or so, with more and more establishments putting the emphasis on serving food rather than merely serving drinks. This has led to the rise of the so-called "gastropub", originally only found in London and the Home Counties (the regions around the capital), but now spread to all parts of the country. The typical gastropub is a sort of British bistro; stylish, blending modern with traditional, and serving a relatively short menu of Modern European/Modern British food. Prices vary enormously and in many places you may spend as much as you would in a smart restaurant.

Beware that the pub-food revolution also means that many pubs with no history of serving food have jumped onto the bandwagon, many with little expertise or knowledge, consequently serving poor-quality overpriced food. Steer clear of pubs offering long menus and complicated dishes, unless they have an established name.

### Pub Hours and Regulations

Pubs' statutory maximum licensing hours were until quite recently: Monday–Saturday 11am–11pm, and Sunday 12.30pm–10.30pm, with many closing during the afternoon. In 2005 "24-hour drinking laws" came into operation allowing the country's pubs, clubs and bars to open, in theory, around the clock. In practice, relatively few premises applied for a licence to extend their hours. Pubs that serve meals (now the majority) normally allow children on the premises as long as they remain within the eating area and even more traditionally inclined pubs may allow children in before a certain time (say 8pm or 9pm). The best policy is to ask someone behind the bar before marching in with kids. You must be 18 to be served with alcohol and, if you look younger, you will almost certainly be asked for some form of age identification.

## Michelin Guide (Red Cover)

The **Michelin Guide Great Britain & Ireland** is an annual publication which presents a selection of hotels and restaurants. All are classified according to the standard of their amenities and their selection is based on regular on-the-spot visits and enquiries. Pleasant settings, attractive décor, quiet or secluded locations and a warm welcome are identified by special symbols. The guide not only celebrates the very best chefs and cuisine that Great Britain has to offer, but also reflects the trend towards informal eating with its Bib Gourmand award to restaurants and other establishments offering good food at moderate prices. Michelin's **Eating Out in Pubs** guide selects the 500 best dining pubs.

### GLOBAL CUISINE

Every town in the UK has its share of Indian and Chinese establishments. Indeed, chicken tikka masala, perhaps the nation's favourite dish, is an Anglo-Indian invention. In places where large Asian immigrant communities have settled (e.g. Bradford or Birmingham) restaurants from the Indian subcontinent are ubiquitous. After years of simply being the cheap option after the pubs closed, many ethnic restaurants have now moved upmarket to enjoy critical acclaim. In the major cities of the United Kingdom you can expect to find the cuisines of almost every country in the world. Increasingly modern Britain, unlike many of her European neighbours, has learned to embrace global cuisine and cooking, even at home.

# Basic Information

## BUSINESS HOURS
## LAST ENTRY TIMES

In the Discovering section of the guide the times we generally give are opening hours; for example, 10am–6pm means the site *closes* at 6pm. In practice many places have a last entry time of 30 minutes to an hour before closing time. If the last entry time is more than an hour before closing time (normally only larger attractions stipulate this) or the attraction specifically states last entry time (as opposed to closing time), we also state this. In genera, however, it is always best to arrive at least 90 minutes before an attraction closes for the day.

## COMMUNICATIONS

Prepaid phonecards, of varying value, are available from post offices and many newsagents; they can be used

| 00 61 | Australia |
|---|---|
| 00 1 | Canada |
| 00 353 | Republic of Ireland |
| 00 64 | New Zealand |
| 00 44 | United Kingdom |
| 00 1 | United States of America |
| 155 | International Operator |

| 100 | Operator |
|---|---|
| 118 500 | BT Directory Enquiries in the UK (£1.50/min, £2.25 minimum charge) |
| 999 | Emergency number (free nationwide); ask for Fire, Police, Ambulance, Coastguard, Mountain Rescue or Cave Rescue |

in booths with phonecard facilities for national and international calls. Some public telephones accept credit cards. Since deregulation a number of telephone operators have set up in competition with the previous state-run British Telecommunications

(BT). Rates vary enormously between operators. For calls made through BT, daytime rates are Mon to Fri, 7am–7pm; evening rates at other times; weekend midnight Friday to midnight Sunday.

## INTERNATIONAL CALLS

To make an international call dial ✆00 followed by the country code, followed by the area code (without the initial 0), followed by the subscriber's number.

## ELECTRICITY

The electric current is 230 volts AC (50 HZ); 3-pin flat wall sockets are standard. An adaptor or multiple point plug is required for non-British appliances.

## EMERGENCIES

Dial **999** and an operator will ask you which service (Police, Fire or Ambulance) you require. These calls are free from any phone.

## MAIL/POST

Post offices are generally open Mondays to Fridays, 9.30am to 5.30pm and Saturday mornings, 9.30am to 12.30pm. Royal Mail pricing is now based on the *size* of a letter as well as the more traditional weight, for example **Postcard/standard** small-letter second-class rate: UK 36p (up to 100g that are no more than 5mm thick and up to C5 in size), Europe 68p, rest of the world 76p. If you are unsure, you will need to  go in person to a post office or visit www.royalmail.com for details. **Stamps** are available from post offices, newsagents and tobacconists, and some supermarkets. **Poste restante** items are held for 14 days; proof of identity is required. **Airmail** delivery usually takes 3 to 4 days in Europe and 4 to 7 days elsewhere in the world.

## MONEY
## BANKS

Banks are generally open from Mondays to Fridays, 9.30am to 3.30pm; some banks offer a limited service on Saturday mornings; all banks are closed on Sundays and bank holidays. Most banks have cash dispensers (ATMs) that accept international credit cards; most do not charge a fee for cash withdrawals (be sure to look for a notice to that effect). Exchange facilities outside these hours are available at airports, currency exchange companies, travel agencies and hotels.

Some form of identification is necessary when cashing travellers' cheques in banks. Commission charges vary; hotels usually charge more than banks.

## CREDIT CARDS

The main credit cards (American Express, Access/Eurocard/Mastercard, Diners Club, Visa/Barclaycard) are widely accepted in shops, hotels, restaurants and petrol stations. Most banks have cash dispensers which accept international credit cards.

## CURRENCY

The official currency in Great Britain is the pound sterling. The decimal system (100 pence = £1) is used throughout Great Britain; Scotland has different notes including £1 and £100 notes, which are legal tender outside Scotland, though you may well have difficulty getting English shopkeepers to accept them; the Channel Islands and Isle of Man have different notes and coins, which are not valid elsewhere.

The common currency – in descending order of value – is £50, £20, £10 and £5 (notes); £2, £1, 50p, 20p, 10p, 5p (silver coins) and 2p and 1p (copper coins). The euro is accepted in some stores in London but check the rate of exchange if planning to make large purchases.

## PUBLIC HOLIDAYS

The table opposite gives the public (**bank**) holidays in England and Wales, when most shops and municipal museums are closed.
In addition to the usual school

| 1 January | New Year's Day |
|---|---|
| **Good Friday** | Friday before Easter Day |
| **Easter Monday** | Monday after Easter Day |
| **First Monday in May** | May Day |
| **Last Monday in May** | Spring Bank Holiday |
| **Last Monday in August** | Bank Holiday |
| **25 December** | Christmas Day |
| **26 December** | Boxing Day |

holidays in the spring and summer and at Christmas, there are half-term breaks in February, May and October.

## SMOKING

It is illegal to smoke in **all** public places, including the (often traditionally smoky) great British pub. Many do, however, provide some kind of outdoor shelter for smokers.

## TAX
### VAT

Many stores in London, Edinburgh and other tourist cities and towns participate in the Retail Export Scheme (look for the sign "Tax-Free Shopping"). This means that customers may be entitled to receive a refund of VAT paid on goods (currently 20 percent) exported to destinations outside the European Union.

There is no statutory minimum sale value although retailers may set a minimum transaction value (normally around £75) below which they will not operate the scheme. Ask the sales assistant for the form for reclaiming the tax.

Fill in the form, keep it safe and present it again at the point of exit from the UK for the refund to be passed on to you. Note that VAT refunds cannot be processed after you return home.

## GIFT AID AND DONATIONS

Gift Aid is a government scheme of tax relief on money donated to UK charities, which since 2007 may be applied at the entrance to visitor attractions with charitable status. The scheme is *only* for UK taxpayers and you will be asked for your postcode and name, which will be verified instantly (electronically) by a machine at the site entrance in order to minimise any waiting time. You will then be given the choice of buying a ticket with or without gift aid. The former is 10 percent higher. Beware that in some cases you may be asked for the gift aid inclusive price straight away, thus putting the onus on you to ask for the cheaper ticket. If so, remember there is absolutely no obligation for you to pay the higher amount (and if you are an overseas visitor the scheme does not apply to you anyway).

In a few instances if you do choose to pay the higher price you may be given an incentive to pay the higher price in the form of a voucher redeemable in the shop, or against refreshments. If you spend the full amount of this voucher (which in most cases will only amount to the price of a coffee or less), then you will pay less overall but the charity/visitor attraction will still gain extra revenue.

Beware also that some historical attractions lead with a price that includes a "charitable donation". You are under no obligation to pay this; simply ask for the standard price ticket instead.

Within this guidebook we have given entry prices *without* gift aid or charitable donations.

## TIME

In winter, standard time throughout the British Isles is Greenwich Mean Time (GMT). In summer clocks are advanced by an hour to give British Summer Time (BST). The actual dates are announced annually but always occur at the weekend in March and October.

Eilean Donan Castle, Highlands, Scotland
© Fantuz Olimpio/Sime/Photononstop

# The Country Today

## 21ST-CENTURY BRITAIN
## POPULATION

*2001 census: 58,789,194 (est 2011 c.60 million)*

Great Britain has long been a cosmopolitan place, shaped by the cultures and peoples that have arrived through invasion, migration, empire and trade, ever since rising sea levels separated the island from mainland Europe. Much of the white population is a hodge-podge of pre-Celtic, Celtic, Roman, Viking, Anglo-Saxon and Norman ancestry. More recent arrivals follow in the shadow of the dwindling memory of the British Empire and the United Kingdom's continuing high profile in international affairs. Alongside increasing movement of citizens within the European Union, all of this ensures that Britain remains a place of change.

It is said that there are around 200 different languages spoken within these shores. Around 8–10 percent of the population is from ethnic minorities, but the concentration of immigrants varies enormously by region and by area. In wealthy rural and semi-rural parts of the country the population is overwhelmingly white, whereas many innercity suburbs of London and provincial cities such as Birmingham and Bradford have substantial communities of other ethnicity.

The United Kingdom has a long history of immigration, with large-scale **European influxes** in the 19thC and early-20thC. After the Second World War many **West Indians** were invited to help with the shortage of labour and they were followed around a decade later by immigrants from **India** and **Pakistan**. There has also been a steady stream of **Chinese**, most notably from the former colony of Hong Kong.

British society is far more integrated than it was 30 years ago, but it is still to some extent insular. Recent statistics indicate that social mobility is not as high as the government has previously hinted.

However, the rigid class divisions of the past have relaxed considerably and equal opportunities continues to be a leading issue. This is perhaps best represented by the huge numbers of students of all classes and ethnicities that join the workforce each year from Britain's government subsidised-universities.

### 21st Century Trends

Since the relaxing of laws on labour movement and the expansion of the European Union, more Europeans (particularly from eastern Europe) have made Britain their home. **Poles** in particular have arrived in large numbers and have been among the most successful at assimilating into the community, largely as a result of their value in the skilled manual labour market.

The recent conflicts and degree of polarisation between the **Muslim** and Christian worlds has exacerbated tensions in some areas of Great Britain, and in some instances radical Muslim clerics have been arrested or expelled from the country. However, the moderate majority, who now account for over 3 percent of the population, flourish in the UK.

**Multiculturalism** is an important political topic in modern Great Britain with an ongoing debate that focuses on balancing the rights and responsibilities of immigrants. On the whole, Britain continues to be a very tolerant society and welcomes most immigrants, though there is also a feeling that the UK has become a "soft touch" for immigrants who contribute little, and the debate is far from clear, whether immigration over recent decades has been good for both the economy and overall quality of life in Great Britain. On a lighter note national polls regularly indicate that the favourite meal on the nation's tables is the British-Indian dish, chicken tikka masala.

Britain continues to be a safe haven for **political refugees** and asylum seekers from several trouble spots of the world. While many residents would like to wash their hands of such problems, others point to the legacy of Empire and the leading role that Great Britain still plays in many parts of the world.

## Being British

By the time the Millennium drew to a close the concept of being British had become increasingly nebulous. The country is now home to immigrants from over 100 different ethnic backgrounds, and many are now second generation, some retaining the garb and traditions of their country but speaking in a broad English regional accent. Sport is the most obvious melting pot where English-born players of Indian fathers play cricket for England against India, while many top British athletes, particularly footballers, are of Afro-Caribbean extraction. Meanwhile, "being British" abroad has taken something of a battering as a result of football hooliganism and the continuing popularity of cheap, boozy holidays by the sea.

With streamlined 21C communications, a growing interest in all things regional (from dialects to food, music and handicrafts), and with fashionable wealthy cities like Cardiff and Edinburgh to call their own, Scotland and Wales are no longer sleepy backwaters to be patronised by London. Of the three mainland British nations it is the English who have suffered the most with regard to their sense of identity. The regionalisation of power to Scotland and Wales (even if the really big decisions are still taken in Whitehall), large-scale immigration, and the demands and legislation of the European Union, have taken their toll on the English national psyche. Meanwhile the Scots and Welsh, with their gleaming new Parliamentary headquarters, have grown in confidence.

## LIFESTYLE

Over the last three decades British lifestyle has become increasingly Americanised with more time spent at work, less time spent on the family, a move from the city to the suburbs, shopping at out-of-town centres rather than in neighbourhood corner shops, and an increasing reliance on the motor car over public transport. Materialism and conspicuous consumption reached its zenith in the late-1980s and early-1990s as typified by "yuppies" (young upwardly mobile professionals) flaunting expensive cars and massive salaries, at least until the recession of the early-90s. The new Millennium boom in London's financial services industry brought enormous City bonuses, while exacerbating a spendthrift consumer culture. All of this came to an abrupt stop in 2008 with the collapse of credit markets around the globe. Economic conditions have been, at best, cautious ever since.

British society has shifted from the relatively tight-knit community structure of the 1950s and 60s to a culture of the individual. While many people have benefited in material terms from the economic boom years, lifestyle changes have had serious implications on the country's physical infrastructure, behaviour and health. Topical debate is dominated by recurring issues of "binge (excessive) drinking", teenage pregnancies, poor childcare, increasing obesity and lack of moral leadership.

## RELIGION

Sunday has long ceased to be the "day of rest", when it was once de rigueur to attend church. The main Sunday pastimes are now shopping and sport. Church attendances in the UK have plummeted to half of what they were 50 years ago and the UK is third from bottom in this respect in the European Union. It is reckoned that only around 15 percent of Britons attend church at least once a month, though it is also estimated that nearly 60 percent still place their faith in Christianity. Of course, with the huge influx of immigration in the UK there are also many other religions now being practised here.

## SPORT

The British have long been a sporting nation, popularising many international sports (football/soccer, golf, cricket, rugby, tennis). Football remains the most popular team game with the English Premier League acknowledged widely as the best (and certainly the richest) in the world. However, its make-up (over 55 percent of players are foreign) is one of the principal reasons for the over hyped

## Paying for the Olympics

The celebrations following the award of the 2012 Olympic Games to London (made in July 2005) were cut short by terrorist bombings the very next day. Ever since, Britain looked forward to the Games with a mixture of hope and apprehension. One of the biggest political questions overshadowing the games was that of legacy. The investment in Olympic facilities will cost taxpayers dearly for generations to come. 2.5 sq km of former industrial, contaminated land in the East End was transformed to create the Olympic Park. Environmental sustainability was at the core of the park's design, but it remains to be seen whether it can sustain the people it was built for, once the games have left.

but under performing English national team, which has failed to win an international tournament since 1966. The influx of foreign players (and coaches) is also now widely felt in other traditional English sports, such as rugby and cricket.

## MEDIA

British media varies from the sublime to the ridiculous, as represented by the "tabloid" (small-format) newspapers, which specialise in deliberately outlandish features and celebrity gossip, garnished with soft porn. Despite claims of "dumbing down" to retain its audience in the face of increasing multi-channel satellite and cable TV competition, the BBC retains its unique licence fee subsidy and maintains a strong presence in global media, underpinned by informative programming and a welcome absence of advertising. The BBC dominates the airwaves with several national radio stations and many more local frequencies, while its investment in the online iPlayer has paid dividends in the longrun, with many users choosing to watch key events, such as Wimbledon tennis, online instead of on TV.

Of the broadsheet newspapers, *The Daily Telegraph*, *The Times*, *The Guardian* and *The Independent* are all good-quality serious daily reads peppered with informed opinion leaning towards the left *(The Guardian)* and the right *(The Daily Telegraph)* with varying shades of politics in between.

"Red-top" tabloid newspapers enjoy far wider circulation and run the gamut of entertainment from the ostentatious headlines of the *Mail on Sunday* to the best selling pages of *The Sun*. The *Daily Mirror*, *Daily Mail* and *Daily Express* are other populist newspapers, each enjoying large readerships nationwide.

## LANGUAGE
### English

The English language owes its rich vocabulary to the many peoples who have

## The Cult of Celebrity

The current British fixation with celebrity really kicked off in the 1980s. It was fuelled by tabloid newspapers, such as The *Sun*, and magazines such as *Hello* which quickly spawned a whole raft of cheap sensationalist "celeb"-spotting titles which now form a mind-boggling display on the racks in high-street newsagents. The groundbreaking "reality televison" programme *Big Brother* came to the UK in 2000. It put members of the general public in a house and simply watched their behaviour and interactions – the more controversial the better – live over many weeks, with its 8-million-strong TV audience voting on who should stay and who should go on a regular basis. The reward for the final "survivor" was a large cash prize and all sorts of media offers to sell their story. Now anyone could be a celebrity, irrespective of talent or achievements.

settled in Great Britain or with whom the British have come into contact through overseas exploration and conquest. Old English's origins are Anglo-Saxon and thus West Germanic, with a peppering of Old Norse (Viking). Middle English was Norman influenced, while Modern English continues to develop and adopt from other languages. In 1600 there were about 2 million English-speakers. The number is now nearer 400 million, including not only the population of countries such as Australia and New Zealand, Canada and the United States of America, but also of those where English is the only common and thus official second language.

**Old English, Anglo-Saxon and Norman French** – Old English, a Germanic dialect spoken in AD 400 from Jutland to northern France, was established in Britain by AD 800 and by the 16C had taken on the syntax and grammar of modern English. Although Norman French was made the official language after the Norman Conquest, Anglo-Saxon eventually gained precedence and Norman French survives principally in formal expressions used in law and royal protocol. It continued to be spoken in the Channel Islands long after it became obsolete in England.

**Modern English** – English is a very flexible language which has readily absorbed a considerable inheritance from Celtic, Roman, Anglo-Saxon, Viking and Norman-French origins. Although the spoken language owes most to Anglo-Saxon, the written language shows the influence of Latin, which for many centuries formed the major study of the educated classes.

Immigration over the past hundred years or so has brought many other languages into everyday use by sizeable communities in Britain. Yiddish-speaking Jews came from Russia in the 19C and early-20C and their German-speaking co-religionists fled from Nazi persecution in the 1930s.

Indians and Pakistanis make up the largest immigrant communities, followed by those born in Germany, the Caribbean and the USA. Generations born here are often bilingual, speaking the mother tongue of their community and current English with the local accent.

## Celtic

Celtic-speakers were pushed westward by the invading Anglo-Saxons and their language was relegated to "second-class" status. Gaelic, as some of the various branches of the Celtic language are now known, is still spoken to some extent in Scotland and Ireland.

Scottish Gaelic declined in status in Lowland Scotland during the medieval period, while the Highland Clearances and teaching of English led to its decline in the Highlands in the 18C–19C.

**Cornish** – This branch of the Celtic languages was the only language of the Cornish peninsula until towards the end of the reign of Henry VIII. Although Dolly Pentreath, who was born in Mousehole in 1686 and died in December 1777, is claimed to be the last speaker of Cornish, there were no doubt other Cornish-speakers, none of whom would have outlived the 18C. Modern efforts to revive the language have had some success.

**Welsh** – In the Statute of Rhuddlan in 1284, Edward I recognised Welsh as an official and legal language. After the Battle of Bosworth in 1485 Welsh nobles hopefully followed the Tudors to London but Henry VIII decreed that "no person shall hold office within the Realme, except they exercise the English speech".

The tradition of poetry and literature in the Welsh language, guarded by the bards and *eisteddfodau*, dates from Taliesin in the 7C. In 1588 the Bible was published in Welsh by Bishop Morgan and it was largely the willingness of the Church in Wales to preach in Welsh which saved the language from extinction. Reading in Welsh was encouraged by the Sunday School Movement, begun in Bala in 1789.

The University of Wales was established in 1893. Teaching in Welsh was introduced in primary schools in 1939 and in secondary schools in 1956. Since 1982

# Traditional Festivals and Festivities

Many rural traditions have declined owing to population mobility, the building over of land once dedicated to festivals and the adoption of new farming methods. On the other hand the popularity of outdoor activities, particularly those connected with sport and horses, has led to many of them evolving into fashionable events in the social calendar.

## Morris Dancing

The origins of Morris dancing are uncertain. According to some the word Morris derives from Moorish. The dancers are traditionally men, dressed in white shirts and trousers, with bells tied below the knee and sometimes colourful hats. Their dances are energetic; for some they carry two handkerchiefs and for others a stout stick which they knock against their partner's stick.

## The Maypole

Until the 17C many parishes had permanent maypoles, pagan fertility symbols belonging to a spring festival, tacitly accepted and tamed by the Christian Church. In 1644, however, under the Puritans, the Maypole was banned throughout England but returned at the Restoration (1660), marking both May Day and Oak Apple Day, 29 May, anniversary of Charles II's entry into London. Permanent maypoles still stand at Barwick-in-Elmet, Yorkshire (80ft/24m) and at Welford-on-Avon (70ft/21m).

## Pancake Day

Shrove Tuesday, the day preceding the first day of Lent, is the occasion for cooking, tossing and eating sweet pancakes, which are served with sugar and lemon juice. Pancake races are held in which the competitors have to run a certain distance tossing a pancake in a frying pan on the way.

## Cheese Rolling

*Parish of Brockworth, Gloucestershire.* A Whit Monday/Spring Bank Holiday festival. A cheese is rolled down a steep slope, with the youth of the village and other nutters allowed to chase after it at the count of three. Injury frequently occurs, but the tradition somehow survives in this generally risk-averse culture. Cheese used to be paraded around the church in Randwick, Gloucestershire, on May Day.

## The Furry Dance

*Helston.* The sole remaining example of a communal spring festival dance in Britain, this dance has taken place in Helston, Cornwall, for centuries, on 8 May, feast day of St Michael the Archangel, patron saint of the church. Despite the thousands of tourists who come to see the dance, it has not changed in character and would be recognisable to any pre-Christian inhabitant of the town.

## Well Dressing

Christianity forbade the worship of water spirits but many wells were simply "purged" and re-dedicated to the Blessed Virgin or one of the saints. In Derbyshire the custom of decking wells or springs with flowers still continues, under the auspices of the Church. Large pictures are formed on boards covered with clay, the design being picked out in flowers, pebbles, shells or any natural object; manufactured materials are not used. It is said that the most famous well dressing, at Tissington, began in its present form either after a prolonged drought in 1615 when only the wells of Tissington continued to give water or in thanksgiving for deliverance from the Black Death (1348–49). St Anne's Well near Buxton is another famous well.

## Eisteddfodau

Wales is famous for its international cultural festivals offering song, music and dance (Builth Wells, Llangollen). Many contestants perform in their national costumes.

## Highland Games

The games, which originated in 11C contests in the arts of war, are held in Scotland between June and September. The heavy events include putting the shot, throwing the hammer and tossing the caber as straight as possible. Other events are athletics, dancing, piping and massed pipe bands.

Channel S4C has broadcast television in the Welsh language.

**Manx** – The language spoken in the Isle of Man was similar to the Gaelic of the Western Isles of Scotland but there has been no viable Manx-speaking community since the 1940s. The present Manx dialect of English shows much influence from Lancashire owing to fishing and tourism in the 19C.

**Scots Gaelic** – In Scotland the Gaelic-speaking area, the *Gàidhealtachd*, is mostly confined to the Western Isles. The language, which was the mother tongue of 50 percent of the population in the 16C, is now spoken by less than 2 percent. The "Normalised" Kings of Scotland, especially David I (1124–53), introduced the Anglo-Norman language and later contact with the English court led to English becoming the language of the aristocracy. After the Union of 1603, the Statute of Iona attempted to impose the teaching of English on the sons of the chiefs and in 1616 the Scottish Privy Council decreed – "that the Inglishe tongue be universallie plantit and the Scotts language, one of cheif and principalle causis of the continewance of barbaritie and incivilitie amongst the inhabitantis of the Ilis and Heylandis, may be abolisheit and removeit".

In 1777 a Gaelic Society was formed in London, the first of many all over the world, which maintain and encourage Gaelic language and literature. The percentage of Gaelic-speakers in Scotland is increasing slowly, particularly in Lowland areas.

### Norn

This Viking language, akin to Icelandic, survived in Orkney and Shetland until the 18C. It was the dominant tongue in Orkney until the Scottish-speaking Sinclairs became Earls of Orkney in 1379 and it remained the language of Shetland until well after the pledging of the Northern Isles to James III of Scotland in 1468–69. Modern dialects of both Shetland and Orkney still contain a sizeable body of words of Norn origin – types of wind and weather, flowers, plants and animals, seasons and holidays. A high percentage of place names throughout the islands are Norn.

## CUISINE

Great Britain provides a cosmopolitan choice of food but also has a rich tradition of regional dishes, all using local fish, game, fruit and dairy products to best advantage. Some of the treats listed below can be hard to find and do not appear in touristy restaurants. You may need to enlist the services of local specialists, such as independent butchers and food shops and farmers' markets in order to track them down.

### London and the Southeast

Steak and kidney pie is chief among the many varieties of pie found. The Kentish marshes nurture fine lamb while Whitstable is famous for its oysters; Dover sole and other fresh fish are available along the coast. Chelsea Buns, dough buns folded round dried fruit, and flavoured with cinnamon, have been enjoyed since Georgian days. Maids of Honour are small puff pastry tarts with ground almond, served almost exclusively at the eponymous tearooms in Kew, next to the famous Royal Botanical Gardens.

### The West Country

Devon and Cornwall are known for clotted cream, served on scones with strawberry jam. It is equally delicious on the apple pies, richly flavoured with cinnamon and cloves, for which the region is renowned. Fresh and potted mackerel are a coastal delicacy, as are pilchards. Cheddar cheese is named after the caves in which it is ripened. Cornwall has given its name to the Cornish pasty, a mixture of beef (skirt), turnip or swede, potatoes and onion baked in a pastry case, shaped like a half-moon, once carried down the region's tin and copper mines, to be eaten at midday.

### Heart of England

The Vale of Evesham is England's fruit growing area – plums and greengages are a speciality, with apples and pears. Herefordshire raises fine beef; the local cider, a refreshing but deceptively potent drink, is used in local dishes, including a pigeon casserole, with cider and orange. Gloucestershire produces excellent cheeses. Worcestershire asparagus, in season, rivals any in flavour, and Worcestershire sauce, a blend of anchovies, garlic, treacle and spices, has been enjoyed worldwide since 1839.

## Thames and Chilterns
Brown Windsor soup made with beef, mutton, carrots and onions is delicious. Aylesbury duck and green peas might be followed by Buckinghamshire (Bucks) cherry bumpers (cherries in shortcrust pastry) or some Banbury apple pie. Breakfasts should always finish with chunky Oxford marmalade on toast.

## East Midlands
Lincolnshire grows fine potatoes and these feature in many dishes particularly with delicate pink, green and white slices of stuffed chine of pork, a piece of back of fat pig, stuffed with green herbs. Three regional cheeses enjoyed countrywide are Stilton, Red Leicester and Derby sage. Bakewell tarts are made of shortcrust pastry with an almond and jam filling. Melton Mowbray pies comprise succulent pork in jelly, with a little anchovy flavouring in a pastry case.

## East Anglia
Norfolk is famed for its dumplings, mussels in cider and mustard. During the summer samphire, "poor man's asparagus", grows wild along the salt marshes and is eaten with melted butter. In Suffolk they serve a spicy shrimp pie, cooked with wine, mace and cloves in a puff pastry case. Cromer crabs and Colchester oysters are excellent.

## Yorkshire, Humberside and the Northeast
Roast beef and Yorkshire pudding – a succulent batter pudding on which the juices of the roasting meat have been allowed to drip – rivals York ham and parkin – a dark oatmeal cake made with cinnamon, ginger, nutmeg and treacle – as Yorkshire's great contribution to British gastronomy. Wensleydale cheese goes well after any of the many game pies or potted grouse for which the area is renowned. Newcastle has potted salmon, and along the Northumberland coast, baked herrings are a delicacy.

## Cumbria and the Northwest
Fish of all sorts from the Irish Sea, cockles, scallops, the smaller flavourful "queenies" from the Isle of Man, potted shrimps in butter, from Morecambe Bay, and Manx kippers are the glory of this region. Char, a fish from the deepwater lakes of the Lake District, is eaten fresh-caught or potted. Cheshire produces two fine cheeses, one white and one a blue vein. Cumberland sauce goes perfectly with ham or game pies.

## Wales
Lamb is traditionally eaten with mint sauce, mutton with redcurrant jelly. Welsh honey lamb is delicious, cooked in cider, with thyme and garlic, basted with honey. Caerphilly produces a light, crumbly cheese. Leeks, the emblem of Wales, appear in many dishes.
A speciality of the Gower is the local sea trout – sewin – stuffed with herbs before being cooked. Welsh cakes and griddle scones with currants are best eaten hot with butter. Bara brith is a rich cake bread, full of dried fruits and citrus peel.

## Scotland
Scottish beef and lamb are renowned, as is Scottish venison, grouse (in season) and salmon. Partan bree is a tasty crab soup and there are Arbroath smokies (smoked haddock) and kippers to rival kedgeree, made with salmon, haddock or other fish, with rice, hard-boiled eggs and butter. Haggis served with swede (the Scots refer to this as turnip or "neeps") is a tasty meal traditionally accompanied by a wee dram of whisky. Mutton pies are made with hot water pastry, and oatmeal bannocks (flat breads) may be spread with local honey. Dundee makes a rich, dark and chunky orange marmalade.

## BEER

Beers in Britain can be divided into two principal types: ales and lagers which differ principally in their respective warm and cool fermentations. Beer is served in kegs or casks.

**Keg beer** is filtered, pasteurised and chilled and then packed into pressurised containers from which it gets its name.

**Cask beer** or "real ale" is neither filtered, pasteurised nor chilled and is served from casks using simple pumps. It is considered to be a more flavoursome and natural beer.

**Bitter** is the traditional beer in England and Wales. Most are a ruddy brown colour with a slightly bitter taste imparted by hops. Some bitters are quite fruity in taste and the higher the alcoholic content the sweeter the brew.

**Mild** is normally only found in Wales, the West Midlands and the Northwest of England. The name refers to the hop character as it is a gentle, sweetish and full-flavoured beer. It is generally lower in alcohol and darker in colour than bitter, caused by the addition of caramel or by using dark malt.

**Stout** can be either dry, as brewed in Ireland (Guinness is the standard bearer) with a pronounced roast flavour with plenty of hoppy bitterness, or sweet. The latter, sweetened with sugar before being bottled, are now rare.

In addition there are **pale ales** (like bitter), brown ales (sweet, like mild) and old ales (sweet and strong) and barley wine, a very sweet, very strong beer.

In **Scotland**, draught beers are often sold as 60/- (shillings), 70/-, 80/- or even 90/-. This is a reference to the now-defunct shilling, which indicated the barrel tax in the late-1800s calculated on alcoholic strength. The 60/- and 90/- brews are now rare.

Alternatively, the beers may be referred to as light, heavy or export which refers to the body and strength.

## WHISKY (WHISKEY)

The term whisky is derived from the Gaelic for "water of life". **Scotch whisky** can only be produced in Scotland, by the distillation of malted and unmalted barley, maize, rye, and mixtures of two or more of these.

**Malt whisky** is produced only from malted barley traditionally dried over peat fires. A single malt whisky comes from one single distillery and has not been blended with whiskies from other distilleries.

The whisky is matured in oak, ideally sherry casks, for at least three years, which affects both its colour and its flavour. All malts have a more distinctive aroma and more intense flavour than grain whiskies and each distillery will produce a completely individual whisky. There are approximately 100 malt whisky distilleries in Scotland.

**Grain whisky** is made from a mixture of any malted or unmalted cereal such as maize or wheat and is distilled in the Coffey, or patent still, by a continuous process. It matures more quickly than malt whisky. Very little grain whisky is ever drunk unblended.

**Blended whisky** is a mix of more than one malt whisky or a mix of malt and grain whiskies to produce a soft, smooth and consistent drink. There are over 2,000 such blends, which form the vast majority of Scottish whisky production.

**Deluxe whiskies** are special because of the ages and qualities of the malts and grain whiskies used in them. They usually include a higher proportion of malts than in most blends.

**Irish whiskey** (note the spelling with an e) is traditionally made from cereals, distilled three times and matured for at least seven years.

## CIDER

Cider has been brewed from apples in Great Britain since Celtic times. Only bitter apples are used for "real" West Country cider, which is dry in taste, flat (non-sparkling) and high in alcoholic content. A sparkling cider is produced by a secondary fermentation.

## WINE

Britain's wine industry has improved by leaps and bounds and there are now several high-quality small vineyards mostly in the south of the country.

## GOVERNMENT

Great Britain is composed of England, Wales, Scotland, the Channel Islands and the Isle of Man. The first three countries are part of the United Kingdom, which also includes Northern Ireland but not the Channel Islands and the Isle of Man, which have their own parliaments and are attached to the Crown.

## MONARCHY

The United Kingdom is a **constitutional monarchy**, a form of government in which supreme power is nominally vested in the sovereign (the king or queen). The origins of monarchy lie in the seven English kingdoms of the 6C–9C – Northumbria, East Anglia, Mercia, Essex, Wessex, Sussex and Kent. Alfred the Great (871–899) began to establish effective rule, but it was Canute (Cnut), a Danish king, who achieved unification. The **coronation** ceremony gave a priestly role to the anointed monarch, especially from the Norman Conquest (1066) onwards. The monarchy became hereditary only gradually. The Wars of the Roses, which dominated the 15C, were about dynastic rivalry and the Tudors gained much from their exploitation of the mystique of monarchy. Although the kingdoms of England and Scotland were united in 1603, the Parliaments were not united until the Act of Union in 1709. The stubborn character of the Stuarts and the insistence of Charles I on the "divine right" of kings was in part responsible for the Civil War and the king's execution, which was followed by the **Commonwealth** (1649–60) under Oliver Cromwell, the only period during which the country was not a monarchy. At the **Restoration** (1660) the monarch's powers were placed under considerable restraints which were increased at the Glorious Revolution (1688) and the accession of William of Orange.

The last vain attempt made by the Stuarts to regain the crown was crushed in the Jacobite risings in 1715 and 1745.

During the reign of Queen Victoria (1837–1901) the monarch's right in relation to ministers was defined as "the right to be consulted, to encourage and to warn", although Victoria clung tenaciously to her supervision of the Empire.

## PARLIAMENT

The United Kingdom has no written constitution. The present situation has been achieved by the enactment of new laws at key points in history. The document known as **Magna Carta** was sealed by a reluctant King John at Runnymede (near Windsor) on 15 June 1215. Clause 39 guarantees every free man security from illegal interference in his person or his property. Since the reign of Henry VII (or perhaps even earlier) "Habeas Corpus" has been used to protect people against arbitrary arrest by requiring the appearance in court of the accused within a specified period. The supreme legislature in the United Kingdom is Parliament, which consists of the **House of Commons** and the **House of Lords**. Medieval Parliaments were mainly meetings between the king and his lords. The Commons were rarely summoned and had no regular meeting place nor even the right of free speech until the 16C. Between 1430 and

### Monarchy in Modernity

In 1997 the death of Diana, Princess of Wales in a car accident in Paris, was the culmination of a series of events (divorces, scandals, revelations) that had rocked the Royal Family and caused the British public to seriously question their validity. However, by the time the Queen celebrated her jubilee year in 2002 most of Britain had regained some sense of loyalty to the institution. But the question of succession remains. Prince Charles treads a fine line between traditionalist and moderniser with a common touch, but his age, and marriage to former lover and divorcee Camilla Parker Bowles, makes many prefer his elder son, Prince William, whose popularity was endorsed by his marriage to Kate Middleton in 2011.

1832 the right to vote was restricted to those possessing a freehold worth 40 shillings. The Reform Act of 1867 enfranchised all borough householders; county householders were included in 1884. In 1918 the franchise was granted to all men over 21 and women over 30; in 1928 the vote was extended to women over 21. Today all over the age of 18 are entitled to vote provided they have entered their names on the electoral roll. Since 1949 the Parliamentary constituencies have been organised on the principle that each should contain about 65,000 voters, which produces 659 Members of the House of Commons. The member elected to represent a constituency is the candidate who receives the largest number of votes. The government is formed by the party that wins the greatest number of seats. The **House of Lords**, at whose meetings the sovereign was always present until the reign of Henry VI, consists of the **Lords Spiritual** (the senior bishops of the Church of England) and the **Lords Temporal** (dukes, marquesses, earls, viscounts and barons). Under the crown, the country is governed by laws which are enacted by the **Legislature** – the two Houses of Parliament – and enforced by the **Judiciary** – the courts of the land.

## ECONOMY
### AGRICULTURE AND FISHING

Until the 18C, the economy of Great Britain was largely agricultural. In the 18C a combination of social and economic conditions led to landowners devoting their wealth and attention to improving land and methods of cultivation, giving rise to the **Agricultural Revolution**. Rapid population growth made it necessary to increase domestic agricultural productivity, as this was before the days of extensive overseas trade of consumables. Land enclosure became increasingly widespread, with even common land being suppressed by Acts of Parliament, landowners arguing that the system of enclosure was better for raising livestock, a more profitable form of agriculture than arable farming. Landowners enlarged their estates by taking over land abandoned by people leaving the countryside for the town, or emigrating to the New World, and developed a system based on maximising profit by introducing many efficient new farming methods. Milestones in this evolution include the use of fertiliser, abandoning the practice of leaving land to lie fallow every three years, and the introduction of new crop varieties (root crops for fodder and cultivated pasture) which in turn fostered the development of stock raising and increasing selectivity.

Nowadays, the average size of a British farm is around 170 acres/69ha, one of the highest figures in Europe. Agriculture, mechanised as much as possible, employs only 2.3 percent of the workforce. The practice of mixed farming, combining stock raising and crop farming, means that modern Britain meets its domestic needs in milk, eggs and potatoes, and almost totally in meat (with a national flock of about 29 million head, the United Kingdom is ninth in the world for farming sheep). The European Union's Common Agricultural Policy has hit British farmers hard, the imposition of quotas forcing them to cut production of milk and adopt less intensive farming methods.

The **fishing industry**, once a mainstay of the island's economy, has declined considerably mainly because of modifications to national fishing boundaries and their attendant fishing rights. Arrangements drawn up for the Anglo-Irish zone and the approved quotas have stabilised the annual catch for UK vessels at around 800,000 tons, but have not succeeded in arresting the decline of once-great fishing ports such as Kingston-upon-Hull or Grimsby after the departure of the canning factories.

### ENERGY SOURCES

**Coal** was mined well before the 18C (Newcastle was exporting 33,000 tons of coal per year as early as the mid-16C), but became a large-scale industry only after the invention of the steam engine. Since the industry's heyday in the early 20C, production has been dropping steadily, despite a brief revival in the 1950s. Nowadays, in the wake of sweeping pit closures, in which deposits were exhausted or where it was felt extraction was no longer profitable, production has dropped significantly.

In 2005 total UK production was 20 million tons, mainly concentrated in Yorkshire and Nottinghamshire. Production figures have not been helped by the fact that the high cost of exploiting most mines means that Britain can import coal more cheaply from countries such as Australia, nor by competition from oil and gas.

In the 1960s prospecting in the **North Sea** gave rise to sufficiently promising results for the countries bordering the sea to reach an agreement, under the Continental Shelf Act of 1964, on zones for extracting **natural gas**. Thanks to deposits along the Norfolk and Lincolnshire coasts, Britain is the world's fifth-largest producer however, domestic demand is so great that gas has to be imported from Norway. Further north, off Scotland and the Shetland Islands, oil deposits give Great Britain further independence in the energy sector, with total crude oil production at 70 million tons in 2007, but still down from 124 million tons in 1998.

Like the majority of developed countries, the United Kingdom converts a large proportion of its primary energy sources into electricity. About 70 percent of the electricity currently produced is thermal in origin (the Drax power station in Yorkshire is the most powerful in Europe). **Hydroelectricity** is negligible, as the relatively flat relief makes it impossible to build any sizeable hydroelectric power stations (only existing stations are in Scotland and Wales).

Nuclear energy, which has evolved since the construction of the experimental reactor at Calder Hall inaugurated in 1956, is produced by a dozen or so nuclear power stations, nearly all of which are to be found on the coast so that they can be cooled adequately. More recently, the wind has been harnessed to produce energy at Burgar Hill in the Orkneys, among other places.

## INDUSTRY

In the second half of the 18C, hot on the heels of the Agricultural Revolution, capital began to flow from the land into industry, with new industrialists using the money from their family's success as cultivators of the land to set up factories, mills and businesses.

The presence of iron ore in Yorkshire, the Midlands and Scotland gave rise to the **iron and steel industry** ( *see Ironbridge Gorge Museum)* which at its peak in the 19C was one of the industries at the core of the country's economy. However, by the beginning of the 20C the mineral deposits were exhausted, and Great Britain found itself importing ore from abroad, effectively bringing about the decline of its own inland iron and steel regions (Durham, the Midlands) in favour of those located on the coast (Teesside) and in South Wales (Port Talbot, Newport). UK steel production is currently at 13–14 million tons per year. Metal processing industries have equally suffered gravely in the face of competition from abroad. There are few remaining large UK **shipyards** operating in the commercial sector, although a large naval shipbuilding programme for the Royal Navy, replacing old aircraft carriers, promises some continuity for the naval yards of Portsmouth, Plymouth, the Clyde, Barrow and Rosyth.

Britain's **car industry** once led Europe, with production levels of 2.3 million vehicles in the mid-1960s. It included some prestigious national companies, such as Triumph, Rover, Jaguar, Bentley and Rolls-Royce. Industrial disputes gave rise to a management crisis, however, culminating in nationalisation (British Leyland in 1975) and privatisation.

In 2004 the UK's automotive industry ranked ninth in the world by size. Japanese firms like Honda, Nissan and Toyota have assembly plants in the UK. VW owns Bentley, Ford owns Aston Martin, while BMW holds a corral of largely defunct British brands, but does produce the Mini (Oxfordshire) and Rolls-Royce cars (Chichester). As of 2008, Tata, an Indian car manufacturer, owns Jaguar Land Rover.

Great Britain has contributed to the rapid evolution of the **electronics and computer industries**. Foreign companies such as Honeywell, Burroughs, IBM, Hewlett-Packard and Mitsubishi have set up business in Scotland, providing a much-needed economic impetus in place of the region's defunct traditional industries. In 2009 the government placed much emphasis on Digital Britain as one of the pillars of the plan to beat the recession, with continuing investment in **communications** and bolstering of **creative industries**.

Great Britain developed a flourishing **textile industry**, thanks to its large numbers of resident sheep and the ground-breaking inventions of the Industrial Revolution, and maintained its position as world leader until the mid-20C. Yorkshire, with Bradford as capital, was home to 80 percent of wool production. Lancashire, with Manchester as its centre, specialised in cotton.

However, this national industry has declined, overtaken by artificial fibres, illustrating the preponderant role that the **chemical industry** now plays in Great Britain's economy. Some of Britain's largest industrial groups are chemical based: Coats Viyella, synthetic fibres; Courtaulds, synthetic fibres, paint and varnish production; ICI, paint, varnish and fertilisers. The largest British chemicals firm is British Petroleum (BP), and two other giants in the field of petrochemicals are supported by an Anglo-Dutch financial association: Shell and Unilever.

## TRADE

Great Britain imports more primary materials than it exports. Services, particularly insurance, banking and business services, account for the largest proportion of GDP, while industry, particularly heavy industry, continues to decline in importance. A reduction in trade with North America has been offset by an increase in volume of trade with European Union member-states, which counts for half of British exports.

Settlement markets, marine and air insurance brokers (Lloyd's, the world's lea-

ding marine risk insurers), life insurance, bank loans, deposits and other financial services combine to make the City of London the world's foremost **financial centre**. The huge profits generated by this business sector and the interest from investments abroad guarantee the United Kingdom's income.

Great Britain was the first European country to emerge from the economic crisis of the late-1980s/early-1990s; and during the second half of the decade and the early part of the Millennium continued to outperform its European neighbours and most other world economies in terms of unemployment rate, inflation and other indicators of economic growth.

The credit freeze resulting from the debt crisis in 2007–08 placed the UK back in recession. This has been met by the government with enormous cash subsidies and controversial quantitative easing' (the creation, if not physical printing, of new money).

# History

Great Britain is positioned at the western edge of Europe, from which it has received successive waves of immigrants who have merged their cultures, languages, beliefs and energies to create an island race which has explored, traded with, dominated and settled other lands all over the world.

## ORIGINS

The ancient history of the British peoples is a melting pot of Celts, Romans, Germanic tribes and Scandinavians.

### THE FIRST SETTLERS

Some 8,000 years ago, Britain, until then part of the greater European land mass, became detached from continental Europe by the rise in sea level caused by retreating glaciers.

Around 5,000 BC the first agricultural peoples arrived and began to transform the landscape into the pattern much as we see today. Having satisfied their survival needs, between 4,000 BC and 1,800 BC they began grander, more spiritually inclined projects such as the construction of Stonehenge and other stone alignments. Around 700 BC saw the arrival of the "**Beaker**" people, who brought a knowledge of metalworking and the Aryan roots of the English language – words such as father, mother, sister and brother.

### THE CELTS

Also around 700 BC Celtic settlers arrived. The **Celts** brought their language, their chariots, the use of coinage and a love of finery, gold and ornaments. Iron swords gave them an ascendancy in battle over the native Britons, estimated at around a million, who were pushed westwards. By 100 BC their lifestyle and customs were well established in Britain. However, the different groups of Celts had only a dialect in common and their lack of any idea of "nationhood" made them vulnerable to the might of Rome.

### THE ROMANS

The **Romans** had no strategic interest in the offshore island of Britannia but the lure of corn, gold, iron, slaves and hunting dogs was enough to entice them to invade. By AD 70 much of the north and Wales had been subdued and 50 or more towns had been established, linked by a network of roads. Rome gave Britain its law and extended the use of coinage into a recognised system, essential to trade in an "urban" society. In 313 Christianity was established as the official religion.

*Hadrian's Wall – Cuddy's Crags near Housesteads Roman Fort*

©Martyn Unsworth/iStockphoto.com

| | |
|---|---|
| **55 BC** | Julius Caesar lands in Britain |
| **AD 42** | Roman invasion of Britain under the Emperor Claudius |
| **61** | Revolt of the Iceni under Queen **Boadicea** |
| **122** | Beginning of the construction of **Hadrian's Wall** |
| **410** | Roman legions withdrawn from Britain following the sack of Rome by Alaric the Goth |

## ANGLO-SAXONS AND VIKINGS

**Saxons** in the form of Germanic mercenaries had manned many of the shore forts of Britain before the final withdrawal of regular Roman troops. As pay became scarce they seized tracts of good farming land and settled permanently.

When St Augustine arrived in Kent in 597, he found that Christianity was already established at the court of King Ethelbert of Kent, whose wife Queen Bertha was a Christian princess. Until the Synod of Whitby in AD 664 the practices of the Roman Church existed side by side with those of the Celtic Church, which had a different way of calculating the date of Easter and a strong and distinctive monastic tradition. The Saxon kingdoms of Britain, which traded as far afield as Russia and Constantinople, were constantly engaged in power struggles not only with one another but also with the Angles and Jutes.

### Viking Invasions

Under the **Vikings**, who took to trading and barter instead of their former piracy, London again became a great trading port, as it had been during the Roman period. By AD 911 eight vassal kings paid homage to King Edgar for almost the whole country. During the disastrous reign of Ethelred, the "Redeless" (lacking wise counsel), England was attacked by Norsemen; in 1013 Swein, King of Denmark, invaded and briefly became king. Ethelred fled to Normandy. His son, Edmund "Ironside", was left to battle against the invaders.

After his murder the Parliament (Witenagemot), preferring strength to weakness, elected the Danish invader

**Canute** (Cnut) as his successor. Seven years after Canute's death Edward, son of Ethelred and his Norman wife, Emma, was chosen to be king.

**Edward the Confessor**, who spent much of his childhood in exile in Normandy, gave land and positions to Normans, who viewed the easy-going English with scarcely concealed contempt. Edward gained popular approval as a devout saintly character, but suffered from rebellious and powerful earls, in particular the Godwins of Wessex.

To guard the southeast shoreline against invasion and pillage Edward the Confessor established the enduring maritime federation known as the **Cinque Ports** (Five Ports), in which Sandwich, Dover, Romney, Hythe and Hastings grouped together to supply ships and men for defence.

As part of his claim to the English throne, his great-nephew, **Duke William of Normandy**, is said to have made Harold, son of Earl Godwin, swear an oath to help William succeed on Edward's death. On 5 January 1066, days after the consecration of his abbey church at Westminster, Edward died, Harold took the throne and the stage was set for a Norman invasion.

| | |
|---|---|
| **449** | First waves of Angles, Saxons and Jutes land in Britain; Hengist and Horsa land at Ebbsfleet in east Kent |
| **597** | **Augustine**, sent by Pope Gregory to convert the British to Christianity, founds a Benedictine monastery in Canterbury |
| **827** | King Egbert of Essex becomes first King of England |
| **851** | Viking raiders winter regularly in Britain and become settlers |
| **871-99** | Reign of **Alfred the Great**, King of Wessex, who contains the Vikings in 871 |
| **911** | Kingdom of Normandy founded by Rollo, a Viking |
| **1016-35** | Reign of **Canute** (Cnut), first Danish King of England |
| **1042-66** | Reign of **Edward the Confessor** |

## FEUDAL ENGLAND

The Norman Conquest solidified England's feudal system from the Battle of Hastings in 1066 onwards. In the following centuries, dynastic struggles were to plague both Britain and the continent.

### NORMANS

The **Normans** were descendants of Norsemen, Vikings, who had settled in northern France in 876. Following the death of Edward the Confessor, Duke William of Normandy, accompanied by some 5,000 knights and followers, invaded England and defeated Harold at the **Battle of Hastings** on 14 October 1066, the last time the country was successfully invaded. Duke William, better known as William the Conqueror, overcame a nation of 1.5–2 million people – descendants of Celts, Romans, Vikings and Saxons – and imposed a strong central authority on a group of kingdoms which ranked among the richest in western Europe.

By the time of the **Domesday Survey** only a handful of English names feature amongst the list of "tenants in chief", revealing a massive shift in ownership of land, and only one of 16 bishops was an Englishman; by 1200 almost every Anglo-Saxon cathedral and abbey, reminders for the vanquished English of their great past, had been demolished and replaced by Norman works. Forty years after the conquest, however, English soldiers fought for an English-born king, **Henry I**, in his French territories.

**1066**   Harold Godwinson defeated at the **Battle of Hastings** by Duke William of Normandy, who is crowned William I in Westminster Abbey on Christmas Day

**1086**   Domesday Survey made by William I to reassess the value of property throughout England for taxation purposes

**1100-35**   Reign of **Henry I**, whose marriage to Matilda of Scots unites the Norman and Saxon royal houses

**1135-54**   Reign of **Stephen**. Henry of Anjou acknowledged as heir to the throne by the Treaty of Winchester

### PLANTAGENETS

**Henry II**, Count of Anjou, married Eleanor, whose dowry brought Aquitaine and Poitou to the English Crown. His dispute over the relative rights of Church and State with Thomas Becket, whom he himself had appointed as Archbishop of Canterbury, led to Becket's murder. Henry's reign deserves to be remembered for the restoration of order in a

Norman motte and bailey

In the immediate post-Conquest years the Normans built timber castles, using an artificial or natural earthen mound ("motte"). A stockaded outer enclosure combined stables, storehouses etc ("bailey"). From c 1150 rebuilding took place in stone.

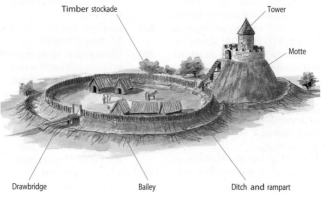

Timber stockade

Tower

Motte

Drawbridge

Bailey

Ditch and rampart

R. Corbel/MICHELIN

## Welsh Marcher Castles

Between 1276 and 1296 17 castles were built or re-fortified by Edward I to consolidate English power in North Wales. The four best-preserved fortresses that once patrolled the North Welsh borders (or Marches) are Conwy, Caernarfon, Harlech and Beaumaris. They are among the most remarkable group of medieval monuments to be seen in Europe.

The four major castles were the work of the greatest military architect of the day, **Master James of St George**, brought by Edward from Savoy. Most were built to be supplied from the sea, as land travel in Snowdonia was impossible for Edward's forces. Square towers were replaced by round, which were less vulnerable to undermining; concentric defences, the inner overlooking outer, made their appearance. The garrisons of these massive stone fortifications were small – only some 30 men-at-arms plus a few cavalry and crossbowmen. Planned walled towns, similar to the "bastides" of southern France, housed the settlers, who helped hold the territory. Documents detailing the conscription of labour from all over England, the costs of timber, stone, transport, a wall, a turret, even a latrine, can still be read.

ravaged country, the institution of legal reforms, which included the establishment of the jury, the system of assize courts and coroners' courts, two reforms of the coinage and the granting of many town charters. He also encouraged the expansion of sheep farming as English wool was of high quality; the heavy

CAERNARFON – A bastide town and castle of the late 13C, North Wales

English kings laid out numerous planned towns ("bastides") to attract settlers and control territory in areas like Gascony and Wales. Though the medieval houses of the English colonists have long since disappeared, Caernarfon retains its castle, its walls and its rectangular street layout.

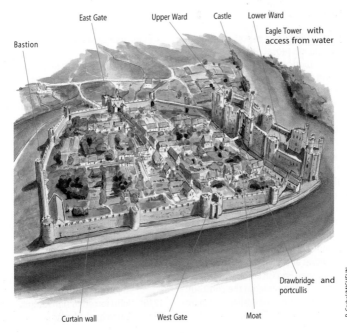

Bastion — East Gate — Upper Ward — Castle — Lower Ward — Eagle Tower with access from water — Curtain wall — West Gate — Moat — Drawbridge and portcullis

R. Corbel/MICHELIN

CAERPHILLY CASTLE, South Wales

A late 13C concentric castle which served as a model for Edward I's strongholds in North Wales

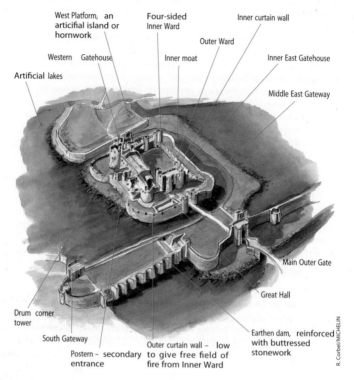

West Platform, an artificial island or hornwork

Four-sided Inner Ward

Inner curtain wall

Western Gatehouse

Outer Ward

Inner moat

Inner East Gatehouse

Artificial lakes

Middle East Gateway

Main Outer Gate

Great Hall

Drum corner tower

South Gateway

Earthen dam, reinforced with buttressed stonework

Postern – secondary entrance

Outer curtain wall – low to give free field of fire from Inner Ward

R. Corbel/MICHELIN

duties levied on its export contributed to England's prosperity.

The despotic manner of ruling and of raising revenue adopted by Henry's son, **King John**, caused the barons to unite and force the king to sign **Magna Carta**, which guaranteed every man freedom from illegal interference with his person or property and the basis of much subsequent English legislation.

The ineffectual reign of John's son, **Henry III**, was marked by baronial opposition and internal strife. He was forced to call the first "parliament" in 1264.

His son, **Edward I**, a typical Plantagenet, fair haired, tall and energetic, was for much of his reign at war with France and Wales and Scotland; on the last two he imposed English administration and justice. During his reign the constitutional importance of Parliament increased; his Model Parliament of 1295 included representatives from shire, city and borough.

His son, **Edward II**, cared for little other than his own pleasure and his reign saw the effective loss of all that his father had won. His wife, Isabel of France, humiliated by her husband's conduct, invaded and deposed Edward.

| | |
|---|---|
| **1154** | Accession of **Henry II**, Count of Anjou (Plantagenet) |
| **1170** | Murder of Thomas Becket in Canterbury Cathedral |
| **1189** | Henry II defeated in battle by his son Richard |
| **1189-99** | Reign of **Richard I** (the **Lionheart**) |
| **1199-1216** | Reign of **King John**. Most of Normandy, Maine, Anjou and Brittany lost |
| **1215** | John forced to sign **Magna Carta** by the barons |

### BODIAM CASTLE, Sussex

Based on French and southern Italian strongholds of the previous century, Bodiam (late 14C) is a perfectly symmetrical square castle, surrounded by a moat and with an array of well-preserved defensive features.

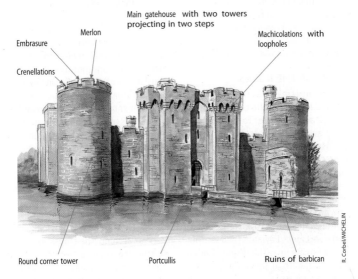

Main gatehouse with two towers projecting in two steps

Merlon

Embrasure

Machicolations with loopholes

Crenellations

R. Corbel/MICHELIN

Round corner tower

Portcullis

Ruins of barbican

| | |
|---|---|
| **1216-72** | Reign of **Henry III**, |
| **1271-1307** | Reign of **Edward I** |
| **1296-98** | North of England ravaged by Scots under **William Wallace**; defeated at Falkirk and executed in 1305 |
| **1307-27** | Reign of **Edward II** |
| **1314** | Edward II defeated at Bannockburn by Robert I, King of Scotland |
| **1327** | Edward II murdered at Berkeley Castle |
| **1327-77** | Reign of **Edward III** |
| **1328** | Robert I recognised as king of an independent Scotland |

## HUNDRED YEARS WAR (1337–1453)

The son of Edward II, **Edward III**, sought reconciliation with the barons and pursued an enlightened trade policy. He reorganised the Navy and led England into the **Hundred Years War**, claiming not only Aquitaine but the throne of France. In 1348 the Black Death plague reached England and the labour force was reduced by one-third.

The throne passed from Edward III to his grandson, **Richard II**, with his uncle,

John of Gaunt, acting as regent. In time Richard quarrelled with the barons. John of Gaunt was exiled together with his son Henry Bolingbroke, who returned to recover his father's confiscated estates, deposed Richard and became king.

**Henry IV** was threatened with rebellion by the Welsh and the Percys, Earls of Northumberland, and with invasion from France.

**Henry V** resumed the Hundred Years War and English claims to the French throne. On his death his infant son was crowned **Henry VI** in 1429 in Westminster Abbey and in 1431 in Notre Dame in Paris.

| | |
|---|---|
| **1337** | Beginning of the **Hundred Years War** with France |
| **1348** | The **Black Death** |
| **1377-99** | Reign of **Richard II** |
| **1381** | Peasants' Revolt, in part provoked by the government's attempt to control wages |
| **1398** | Richard II deposed by Henry Bolingbroke |
| **1399-1413** | Reign of **Henry IV** |
| **1400** | Death of Richard II |
| **1413-22** | Reign of **Henry V** |

**1415** English defeat French at Battle of Agincourt

**1420** Treaty of Troyes makes Henry V heir to the French throne

**1422-61** Reign of **Henry VI** with Duke of Gloucester and Duke of Lancaster as regents

**1453** Hundred Years War ends

## WARS OF THE ROSES

The regency created by the deposing of Edward II fostered the counter-claims of York and Lancaster to develop into the **Wars of the Roses**. The Lancastrians (**Henry IV**, **Henry V** and **Henry VI**), represented by the red rose of Lancaster, claimed the throne by direct male descent from John of Gaunt, fourth son of Edward III. The Yorkists (**Edward IV**, **Edward V** and **Richard III**), represented by the white rose of York, were descended from Lionel, Edward's third son, but in the female line. The dispute ended when Elizabeth of York married Henry Tudor, a Lancastrian.

Edward V and his younger brother, Richard, known as the **Little Princes in the Tower**, were imprisoned by their uncle Richard, Duke of Gloucester. Their claim to the throne was deemed illegitimate by Parliament. Gloucester was proclaimed **Richard III** and the princes were probably murdered at the Tower of London.

**1455-87** **Wars of the Roses**, over 30 years of sporadic fighting and periods of armed peace, between the houses of Lancaster and York, rival claimants to the throne

**1461-83** Reign of **Edward IV**

**1465** Henry VI captured and imprisoned in the Tower of London

**1470** Restoration of Henry VI by Warwick and flight of Edward

**1471** Murder of Henry VI and Prince Edward by Edward IV following his victory at Tewkesbury

**1483** Reign of **Edward V** ending in his and his brother's imprisonment in the Tower of London

**1483-85** Reign of **Richard III**

**1485** Battle of Bosworth Field: Richard defeated and killed by Henry Tudor

## ABSOLUTE MONARCHY

The Renaissance period witnessed the growing conflicts between royalty and other institutions (notably the Church and Parliament). The Tudors in the 16thC and the Stuarts in the 17thC were the embodiment of absolute monarchy. This period was also all about the struggle between the Catholic, Protestant and Anglican churches and communities.

## TUDORS

**Henry VII** ruled shrewdly and his control of finances restored order and a healthy Treasury after the Wars of the Roses.

His son, **Henry VIII**, was a "Renaissance Man", an accomplished musician, linguist, scholar and soldier. He was an autocratic monarch of capricious temper and elastic conscience, who achieved union with Ireland and Wales and greatly strengthened the Navy. Thomas Wolsey, appointed Chancellor in 1515, fell from favour for failing to obtain papal approval for Henry to divorce Catherine of Aragon; his palace at Hampton Court was confiscated by the king. The **Dissolution of the Monasteries** caused the greatest redistribution of land in England since the Norman Conquest. Wool, much of which had been exported raw in the previous century, was now nearly all made into cloth at home.

The popularity of **Mary**, daughter of Henry VIII and Catherine of Aragon, was undermined by her insistence on marrying Philip II of Spain, who was a Roman Catholic, the burning of 300 alleged heretics, and war with France, which resulted in the loss of Calais, England's last possession in continental Europe.

**Elizabeth I**, daughter of Henry VIII and Anne Boleyn, restored a moderate Anglicanism, though potential Roman Catholic conspiracies to supplant her were ruthlessly suppressed. She sought to avoid the needless expense of war by diplomacy and a network of informers controlled by her Secretaries, Cecil and

Walsingham. Opposition to Elizabeth as queen focused on **Mary Queen of Scots** and looked to Spain for assistance. The long struggle against Spain, mostly fought out at sea, culminated in the launch of the Spanish Armada, the final and unsuccessful attempt by Spain to conquer England and re-establish the Roman Catholic faith; its defeat was the greatest military victory of Elizabeth I's reign. Elizabeth I presided over a period of exploration and enterprise, a flowering of national culture and the arts; most of **William Shakespeare**'s greatest plays were produced between 1592 and 1616.

| | |
|---|---|
| **1485-1509** | Reign of **Henry VII** |
| **1509-47** | Reign of **Henry VIII** |
| **1513** | Defeat and death of James IV of Scotland at Flodden |
| **1535** | Execution of Sir Thomas More, Chancellor, for refusing to sign the Act of Supremacy, acknowledging Henry VIII as head of the Church in place of the Pope |
| **1536-39** | Dissolution of the Monasteries. Excommunication of Henry VIII |
| **1547-53** | Reign of **Edward VI** |
| **1553-58** | Reign of **Mary I**; Roman Catholicism re-established |
| **1558-1603** | Reign of **Elizabeth I** |
| **1567-1625** | Reign of James VI, King of the Scots |
| **1580** | Circumnavigation of the world by **Francis Drake** |
| **1587** | Execution of Mary Queen of Scots |
| **1588** | Defeat of the Spanish Armada |

## STUARTS

Elizabeth I was succeeded by **James I** of England and VI of Scotland. The **Gunpowder Plot** was a conspiracy of Roman Catholics who attempted to assassinate James in Parliament, despite his willingness to extend to them a measure of toleration.

**Charles I** inherited his father's belief in an absolute monarchy – the "divine right of kings" – and attempted to rule without Parliament from 1626 to 1640.

Moreover, his marriage to a Roman Catholic, Henrietta Maria of France, was unpopular with the people. When he was finally forced to recall Parliament, the Members of the House responded by condemning his adviser, the Earl of Strafford, to death for treason, refusing to grant the king money until he discussed their grievances, and they passed a Bill preventing any future dissolution of Parliament without their consent. When in 1642 Charles I attempted to arrest five members of Parliament he sowed the final seeds for the coming conflict.

| | |
|---|---|
| **1603-25** | Reign of **James I** (also James VI of Scotland) |
| **1605** | Gunpowder Plot intended to assassinate the king in Parliament |
| **1620** | Pilgrim Fathers set sail for America |
| **1625-49** | Reign of **Charles I** |
| **1626** | Dissolution of Parliament by the king |

## THE ENGLISH CIVIL WAR

The **English Civil War** broke out in August 1642. Charles I established his headquarters in Oxford but the balance was tilted against him by Scots support for the Parliamentarians. The North was lost after the Battle of Marston Moor in 1644 and, following the formation of the **New Model Army** by **Cromwell** and **Fairfax** and its victory at Naseby in 1645, the Royalists surrendered at Oxford the following year. The king surrendered to the Scots who handed him over to Parliament in 1647. A compromise was attempted but Charles wavered. He played off one faction in Parliament against another and sought finance and troops from abroad. In 1648 the war resumed. The Scots to whom Charles promised a Presbyterian England in return for their help, invaded England but were defeated in August at Preston and Charles I was captured. The army demanded his death.

Under the **Commonwealth and Protectorate** the monarchy and the House of Lords were abolished and replaced by a Council of State of 40 members.

Attempts by the "Rump" Parliament to turn itself into a permanent non-elected body caused Cromwell to dissolve it and form the Protectorate in 1653, in which he, as Lord Protector, ruled by decree. He was accepted by the majority of a war-weary population but, on his death in 1658, the lack of a competent successor provoked negotiations which led to the Restoration of the Monarchy.

**1649**   Trial and execution of the king
**1649**   Beginning of the **Commonwealth**. England is ruled not by a monarch but by Oliver Cromwell, a commoner
**1651**   Coronation at Scone of Charles II. He is defeated at the Battle of Worcester and flees to France.

## THE RESTORATION

The **Restoration** in May 1660 ended 10 years of Puritan restriction and opened a period of optimism and a flourishing of theatre, painting and the arts. In the Declaration of Breda Charles II appeared to promise something for almost every political faction. The **Navigation Acts**, specifying that English goods must be carried in English ships, did much to develop commerce.

In 1685, just after the death of Charles II, his illegitimate son, the Duke of Monmouth, whom he had refused to legitimise, led a rebellion against James II, which was brutally repressed. This and the introduction of pro-Catholic policies, two Declarations of Indulgence in 1687 and 1688, the trial and acquittal of the Seven Bishops and the birth of a son James, who became the "Old Pretender", all intensified fears of a Roman Catholic succession. Disaffected politicians approached William of Orange, married to Mary, James' daughter, and offered him the throne.

**1660-85**   Reign of **Charles II**
**1665**   **Great Plague** in which more than 68,000 Londoners died
**1666**   **Great Fire of London** destroys 80 percent of the city

**1672**   Declaration of Indulgence relaxing penal laws against Roman Catholics and other dissenters
**1672-74**   War against the Dutch
**1673**   Test Act excluding Roman Catholics and other non-conformists from civil office
**1677**   Marriage of Charles II's niece, Mary, to William of Orange
**1679**   Habeas Corpus Act reinforcing existing powers protecting individuals against arbitrary imprisonment
**1685-88**   Reign of **James II**
**1685**   Monmouth Rebellion – unsuccessful attempt to claim the throne by the Duke of Monmouth, illegitimate son of Charles II
**1687**   Dissolution of Parliament by James II

## THE GLORIOUS REVOLUTION

**William III** landed in England in 1688. In 1689 he was crowned with his wife Mary as his queen. Jacobite supporters of the exiled James II were decisively defeated in both Ireland and Scotland and much of William's reign was devoted, with the Grand Alliance he formed with Austria, the Netherlands, Spain and the German states, to obstructing the territorial ambitions of Louis XIV of France.

**Queen Anne**, staunch Protestant and supporter of the Glorious Revolution (1688), which deposed her father, James II, also strove to reduce the power and influence of France in Europe and to ensure a Protestant succession to the throne. Marlborough's victory at Blenheim and his successes in the Low Countries achieved much of the first aim. After 18 pregnancies and the death of her last surviving child in 1701, Anne agreed to the **Act of Settlement** providing for the throne to pass to Sophia, Electress of Hanover, grand daughter of James I, or to her heirs.

The "**Whigs**" were the members of the political party which had invited William to take the throne. They formed powerful juntas during the reigns of William and Anne and ensured the Hanoverian succession. In the 1860s they became the Liberal Party. The **"Tories"** accepted the Glorious Revolution but became associated with Jacobite feelings and were out of favour until the new Tory party, under Pitt the Younger, took office in 1783. They developed into the Conservative Party under Peel in 1834.

The **Jacobites**, supporters of the Stuart claim to the throne, made two attempts to dethrone the Hanoverian George I. James II's son, the "Old Pretender", led the first Jacobite rising in 1715 and his eldest son, Charles Edward Stuart, "Bonnie Prince Charlie", the "Young Pretender", led a similar rising in 1745, which ended in 1746 at Culloden, the last battle fought on British soil. He died in exile in 1788 and his younger brother died childless in 1807.

| 1688 | William of Orange invited to England. Exile of James II to France |
| 1689-94 | Reign of **William III and Mary II** |
| 1689 | Defeat of Scottish Jacobites at Killiecrankie. Londonderry besieged by James II; Grand Alliance between England, Austria, the Netherlands and German states in war against France |
| 1690 | Battle of the Boyne and defeat of James II and the Irish Jacobites |
| 1694-1702 | Reign of **William III** following the death of Mary II |
| 1694 | Triennial Act providing for Parliament to meet at least once every three years and to sit for not more than three years |
| 1694 | Bank of England founded |
| 1695 | Bank of Scotland founded |
| 1702-14 | Reign of **Queen Anne** |

## BRITISH EMPIRE

With the battles between Parliament and the monarchy concluded, maritime supremacy established and industrial output exploding, Britain focused on international trade and colonisation.

## HANOVERIANS

By the time **George I** ascended the throne in 1714, the United Kingdom was already a European economic and naval power which had played a major part in weakening the influence of France in Europe.

**George II** is notable for being the last monarch to command his forces personally in battle, at Dettingen in 1743 in the war of the Austrian Succession.

He was succeeded by his grandson, the unfortunate **George III**, prone to bouts of apparent madness (possibly due to porphyria or arsenic poisoning). He was unable to reverse the trend towards constitutional monarchy but he did try to exercise the right of a king to govern. This caused great unpopularity, and he was forced to acknowledge the reality of party politics. Foreign policy was dominated by the king's determination to suppress the American Revolution and the **Napoleonic Wars**, which arose from the threat posed by the Revolution in France to established European powers.

**George IV** had supported the Whig cause as a symbol of opposition to his father's Tory advisers and was much influenced by the politician Charles James Fox.

**William IV** was 65 when he succeeded his unpopular brother. Dissatisfaction with Parliamentary representation was near to causing revolutionary radicals to join forces with the mob.

| 1704 | Gibraltar captured by the English; English victory at Blenheim |
| 1707 | Act of Union joining the Parliaments of England and Scotland |
| 1714-27 | Reign of **George I** |
| 1715 | Jacobite rebellion, led by James Edward Stuart, the Old Pretender |
| 1727-60 | Reign of **George II** |
| 1745 | Jacobite rebellion led by Bonnie Prince Charlie, the Young Pretender, which ended at Culloden in 1746 |
| 1752 | Gregorian Calendar adopted |

*Queen Victoria*

A. Taverner/MICHELIN

Napoleonic Wars both stimulated this industrialism and aggravated the unrest but by the mid-19C it was clear that in Britain industrial revolution would not be followed by political revolution.

| | |
|---|---|
| 1731 | Agriculture revolutionised by the invention of the horse hoe and seed drill by Jethro Tull |
| 1733 | Invention of the flying shuttle by John Kay |
| 1769 | Patents issued for Watt's steam engine and Arkwright's water frame |
| 1781 | Patent issued for Watt's steam engine for rotary motion |
| 1787 | Invention of the power loom by Cartwright |
| 1825 | Opening of the Stockton and Darlington railway. Completion of the Menai Bridge by Telford |
| 1833 | Factory Act abolishes child labour |
| 1834 | Tolpuddle Martyrs transported to Australia for forming an agriculture Trade Union |
| 1851 | Great Exhibition in the Crystal Palace in Hyde Park |
| 1856 | Invention of the Bessemer process of steel making in industrial quantities |

| | |
|---|---|
| 1756 | Beginning of the Seven Years War. Ministry formed by Pitt the Elder |
| 1757 | Recapture of Calcutta. Battle of Plassey won by Clive |
| 1759 | Defeat of the French army by General Wolfe on the Heights of Abraham, Quebec |
| 1760-1820 | Reign of **George III** |
| 1760 | Conquest of Canada |
| 1763 | Seven Years War ended in the Treaty of Paris |
| 1773 | **Boston Tea Party**, a protest against forced imports of cheap East India Company tea into the American colonies |
| 1776 | American Declaration of Independence; *The Wealth of Nations* published by Adam Smith |
| 1781 | British surrender at Yorktown |
| 1793 | War against Revolutionary France |
| 1799 | First levy of income tax to finance the war |
| 1805 | Naval victory at Trafalgar and death of Nelson |
| 1807 | Abolition of the slave trade within the British Empire |

## INDUSTRIAL REVOLUTION

Vast social changes occurred as the labour force moved from the land into town; overcrowding often bred unrest between worker and employer. The

## THE VICTORIAN ERA

As William IV's two daughters had died as infants, he was succeeded on his death by his niece, Victoria.

Queen **Victoria**, the last monarch of the House of Hanover, was only 18 when she came to the throne. She went on to become Britain's longest-reigning sovereign and to give her name to an illustrious age. Her husband, the **Prince Consort, Albert of Saxe-Coburg**, was her closest adviser until his premature death in 1861. He persuaded her that the crown should not be aligned with any political party – a principle that has endured. He was the instigator of the **Great Exhibition**, which took place between May and October in 1851. It contained exhibits from all nations and was a proud declaration of the high point of the Industrial Revolution,

## Welsh History

The character of modern Wales was first formed by the **Romans**, who pushed the Britons west into the land area now known as Wales. It was then a number of kingdoms, rarely united by any single ruler. Mercia (corresponding to today's Midlands) became the dominant **Anglo-Saxon** kingdom and built Offa's Dyke as the Welsh border. When William I conquered Britain in 1066, he halted his advance here. Although the English kings and Welsh leaders had fought for centuries it was **Edward I** who led the first conquest of Wales in 1277, securing the lands with his famous castles, at Harlech, Caernarfon, Conwy, Beaumaris and elsewhere. In the late-18C the **Industrial Revolution** transformed South Wales. The presence of iron ore, limestone and large coal deposits in southeast Wales meant that this region was ideal for the establishment of iron and steel works and coal mines. By 1830, Britain was the largest iron producer in the world, and South Wales alone accounted for 40 percent of this output. Cardiff was soon among the most important coal ports in the world and Swansea among the most important steel ports. The iron and steel industry was not to last, however, as ore was exhausted and other countries took advantage of the new technologies. By the end of the 19C, iron production was in decline and coal was king in South Wales.

The **coal industry** reached its zenith in the 1920s with over a quarter of a million miners working in over 600 coalfields providing one-third of the world's coal. Exhaustion of the seams, underinvestment in the pits, and the recession of the 1930s meant that only half of these were still operating by the outbreak of the Second World War. Pit closures became an acrimonious political issue in the 1980s and resulted in the bitter and ultimately disastrous miners' strike of 1984–85. Today every pit of any reasonable size and everyfoundry has gone.

Despite the gloom of the recent past, Wales in the 21C looks forward to a brighter future with its own Parliament, a renewed interest in the language, national identity and massive urban regeneration projects at Cardiff, Swansea, Llanelli and Ebbw Vale.

celebrating the inventiveness, technical achievement and prosperity which are the hallmarks of the Victorian Age. Her son, **Edward VII**, who was excluded from royal duties and responsibilities until 1892, greatly increased the prestige of the monarchy by his own charm and by reviving royal public ceremonial.

**1812-14** Anglo-American War ended by Treaty of Ghent

**1815** Battle of Waterloo; defeat of Napoleon; Congress of Vienna

**1820-30** Reign of **George IV**

**1823** Reform of criminal law and prisons by Peel

**1829** Catholic Emancipation Act. Formation of the Metropolitan Police

**1830-37** Reign of **William IV**

**1832** First Parliamentary Reform Act

**1837-1901** Reign of **Victoria**

**1840** Marriage of Victoria to Prince Albert. Introduction of the penny post

**1842** Chartist movement campaigns for Parliamentary reform

**1846** Repeal of the Corn Laws

**1848** Cholera epidemic. Public Health Act

**1854-56 Crimean War**, ends with the Treaty of Paris

**1857** Indian Mutiny

**1858** Government of India transferred from the East India Company to the Crown

**1861** Death of Prince Albert

**1863** Opening of the first underground railway in London, the Metropolitan Railway

**1871** Bank holidays introduced

**1876** Victoria made Empress of India. Elementary education made obligatory

# Scientific Progress

**Between 1760 and 1850 the Industrial Revolution turned Britain into the world's first industrial nation. Power-driven machines replaced human muscle and factory production replaced cottage industry. New methods and new machines supplied expanding markets and growing demand.**

## Power

In 1712 **Thomas Newcomen** designed the first practical piston and steam engine and his idea was later much improved by **James Watt**. Such engines were needed to pump water and to raise men and ore from mines and soon replaced waterwheels as the power source for the cotton factories which sprang up in Lancashire. Then **Richard Trevithick** (1771–1833), Cornish tin miner, designed a boiler with the fire box inside which he showed to **George Stephenson** (1781–1848) and his son, **Robert** (1803–59). This became the basis of the early "locomotives".

Without abundant coal, however, sufficient iron could never have been produced for all the new machines. By 1880, 154 million tons of coal were being transported across Britain. Cast iron had been produced by Shropshire ironmaster **Abraham Darby** in Coalbrookdale in 1709 and was used for the cylinders of early steam engines and for bridges and aqueducts. Wrought iron with greater tensile strength was developed in the 1790s, allowing more accurate and stronger machine parts, railway lines and bridging materials. In 1856 **Sir Henry Bessemer** devised a system in which compressed air is blown through the molten metal, burning off impurities and producing a stronger steel.

## Transport

**Thomas Telford** (1757–1834) built roads and bridges for the use of stagecoaches and broad-wheeled wagons transporting people and goods. However, these were often impassable in winter so cheap transport for bulk goods was also provided by over 4,000mi/6,400km of canals, pioneered by **James Brindley** (1716–72). Eventually heavy goods and long-distance passenger traffic passed to the railways.

Engineered by **George Stephenson** (of in 1825, the Stockton and Darlington Railway was the first passenger-carrying public steam railway in the world, by 1835 the railway had become the vital element of the Industrial Revolution – swift, efficient and cheap transport for raw materials and finished goods. The success of Stephenson's *Rocket* proved the feasibility of locomotives. **Isambard Kingdom Brunel** (1806–59), Chief Engineer to the Great Western Railway, designed the Clifton Suspension Bridge and also the first successful trans-Atlantic steamship, the *Great Western*, in 1837.

**William Henry Morris** – Lord Nuffield, the most influential of British car manufacturers, began with bicycles and made his first car in 1913. He is probably best remembered for his 1959 "Mini".

**John Boyd Dunlop** started with bicycles too. In 1888 this Scottish veterinary surgeon invented the first pneumatic tyre. It was **John Loudon McAdam**, an Ayrshire engineer, who devised the "Tarmacadam" surfacing for roads. More recently **Christopher Cockerell** patented a design for the first hovercraft in 1955.

## Aviation

The names of **Charles Rolls** and **Henry Royce** will always be associated with the grand cars they pioneered although their contribution to aviation is arguably even greater. A Rolls-Royce engine powered Sir Frank Whittle's Gloster E28/29, the first jet aircraft, and the De Havilland Comet, the world's first commercial passenger-carrying jet airliner, which made its maiden flight in 1949. British aerospace designers worked with their French counterparts in the development of Concorde, the world's first supersonic airliner.

## Science

In 1660 Sir **Francis Bacon** (1561–1626) founded the Royal Society; it was granted a Charter by Charles II in 1662 "to promote discussion, particularly in the physical sciences". **Robert Boyle** and **Sir Christopher Wren** were founder members and Sir Isaac Newton was its president from 1703 to 1727. **Michael Faraday** was appointed assistant to Sir Humphrey Davy, inventor of the miners'

Safety Lamp, in 1812. It was Faraday's work with electromagnetism which led to the development of the electric dynamo and motor. An early form of computer, the "difference engine" was invented by **Charles Babbage** in 1833 and can be seen in the library of King's College, Cambridge. **Edmond Halley**, friend of Newton, became Astronomer Royal in 1720. He is best remembered for the comet named after him, and for correctly predicting its 76-year cycle and return in 1758.

The radio telescope at Jodrell Bank, set up by **Sir Bernard Lovell** in 1955, is still one of the largest in the world and contributes to our widening knowledge of our Universe. In 1968 **Antony Hewish**, a British astronomer at Cambridge, first discovered pulsars, cosmic sources of light or radio energy. In 1988 **Professor Stephen Hawking** studied black holes and wrote his seminal treatise, *A Brief History of Time*.

## Medicine

It was **William Harvey**, physician to James I and Charles I, who discovered the circulation of the blood. More recent British achievements in medicine have been those of Dr Jacob Bell who, with Dr Simpson from Edinburgh, introduced chloroform anaesthesia, which met with public approval after Queen Victoria used it during the birth of Prince Leopold in 1853. **Sir Alexander Fleming** discovered the effects of penicillin in killing bacteria in 1928. The "double-helix" structure of DNA (de-oxy-ribo-nucleic acid) – the major component of chromosomes which carry genetic information and control inheritance of characteristics – was proposed by Francis Crick working at the Cavendish Laboratory in Cambridge, with his American colleague, James Watson, in 1953. The cloning of Dolly the sheep, in 1996, by the Roslin Institute in Scotland marked a new era in genetic engineering.

## Natural History

**John Tradescant** and son were gardeners to Charles I and planted the first physic (medicinal plant) garden in 1628, leading to the remarkable Chelsea Physic Garden, founded in 1673, open to the public today. **James Hutton** (1726–97) wrote a treatise entitled *A Theory of the Earth* (1785), which forms the basis of modern geology.

**Sir Joseph Banks** (1743–1820), botanist and explorer, accompanied James Cook's expedition round the world in *Endeavour* (1768–71) and collected many previously unknown plants. Together with the biologist Thomas Huxley (1825–95), they supported the pioneering research of **Charles Darwin** (1809–1882), the father of the theory of evolution outlined in his famous work, *On the Origin of Species*, which had a great impact on the study of natural sciences.

## Exploration

Maritime exploration spurred on by the enquiring spirit of the 16C led to the discovery of new worlds. Following the voyages of Portuguese explorers, **John Cabot**, a Genoese settled in Bristol, discovered Nova Scotia and Newfoundland. Rivalry between England and Spain and other European nations in search of trade, as well as scientific advances in navigational aids and improvements in ship construction, led to an explosion of maritime exploration. English mariners included: John Hawkins (1532–95), who introduced tobacco and sweet potatoes to England; **Sir Francis Drake** (c1540–96), the first Englishman to circumnavigate the world; **Sir Walter Raleigh** (1552–1618), who discovered Virginia; Martin Frobisher, who explored the North Atlantic and discovered Baffin Island (1574). Hudson Bay in Canada is named after the explorer Henry Hudson (1610). Captain **James Cook** (1728–79) explored the Pacific, and charted the coasts of Australia and New Zealand and surveyed the Newfoundland coast. Other famous explorers include **Mungo Park** (1771–1806), who explored West Africa and attempted to trace the course of the Niger River; **David Livingstone** (1813–73), a doctor and missionary who campaigned against the slave trade and was the first to cross the African mainland from east to west and discovered the Victoria Falls and Lake Nyasa (now Lake Malawi); Alexander Mackenzie (1755–1820), the first man to cross the American continent by land (1783); and John McDouall Stuart (1815–66), who explored the Australian desert.

**1884** Invention of the steam turbine by Parsons

**1888** Local Government Act establishing county councils and county boroughs

**1895** First Motor Show in London

**1899–1902** Boer War ends in the Peace of Vereeniging, leading to union of South Africa (1910)

## 20TH–21ST CENTURY

Following the two world wars Great Britain took its place at the top table of the free world. At the second decade of the 21C approaches, Britain's military powers may have diminished, but it remains a key player in world politics.

### WORLD AT WAR

The assassination of Archduke Ferdinand at Sarajevo in 1914 plunged Europe (and beyond) into a futile stalemate war in which a million British troops died and many millions more lost their lives. Meanwhile in Ireland a desire for independence had also reached crisis point and in Easter 1916 an uprising in Dublin was ruthlessly put down by British troops.

A significant after-effect of the First World War in Great Britain was a loosening of **class structure**. The "lions led by donkeys" were now much less likely to follow orders in peacetime and the Labour Party made great strides, coming to power for the first time (albeit in a Liberal coalition) in 1923.

Across the water in Ireland the independence movement was continuing and in 1921 an Irish Free State was created. It led to the Irish Civil War, which ended in 1923.

In Britain the **General Strike** of 1926 underlined the country's growing restlessness and this unrest worsened in the 1930s, as the worldwide economy slumped into the Great Depression.

### Second World War

A policy of appeasement was taken towards the growing ambitions of Adolf Hitler, characterised by Prime Minister Neville Chamberlain in 1938, who returned from a meeting with the Führer and delivered the now-infamous words 'I believe it is peace in our time'. When it became clear, however, in 1939, with the invasion of Poland, that war was the only option for Britain, the country found itself seriously unprepared. By mid-1940 Britain was isolated and prepared to be invaded by Hitler's army from across the Channel.

The evacuation of troops at Dunkirk was the nadir. The tide, however, was about to turn. In May **Winston Churchill** became prime minister and the **Battle of Britain** had halted the Luftwaffe's ambitions. This led to the **Blitz** over London and other major cities, in the autumn and winter of 1940–41. In 1941 the **United States** entered the war and the Germans became disastrously entrenched on the **Eastern Front** in Russia. By 1944 the German armies were in retreat and the **Normandy (D-Day) Landings** spearheaded the liberation of Europe.

Coronation of Elizabeth II at Westminster Abbey, 2nd June 1953

©UPPA/Photoshot

**1900** Labour Party formed

**1901-10** Reign of **Edward VII**

**1903** Women's suffrage movement started by Mrs Pankhurst

**1905** First motor buses in London

**1910-36** Reign of **George V**

**1914-18** First World War

**1914** Formation of Kitchener's "Volunteer Army"

**1916** Easter Rising in Dublin

| | |
|---|---|
| **1917** | Name of the Royal Family changed to Windsor by George V |
| **1918** | Women over 30 granted vote |
| **1919** | Treaty of Versailles |
| **1921** | Creation of the Irish Free State |
| **1924** | British Empire Exhibition |
| **1926** | General Strike |
| **1928** | Women over 21 granted vote |
| **1931** | **The Depression** – many people out of work |
| **1936** | Accession and abdication of **Edward VIII** |
| **1936-52** | Reign of **George VI** |
| **1939-45** | **Second World War** |
| **1940** | **Winston Churchill** becomes prime minister |
| **1940** | Evacuation of Dunkirk; **Battle of Britain** |
| **1944** | **Normandy landings** |

## POST-WAR BRITAIN

The years following the Second World War marked the end of the British Empire. In most cases this was a peaceful transition. India achieved independence in 1947 and within the next 10 years virtually all of Britain's overseas dependencies followed suit, changing into the **British Commonwealth**, an informal non-political union which fosters economic cooperation and best practices between member nations.

After 1945 key industries were nationalised and the **Welfare State** was born with the National Health Service, improved pensions and benefits.

**Elizabeth II**, who succeeded to the throne in 1952, has done much to strengthen the role of monarchy both at home and abroad and even following the royalty's recent troubled years the Queen remains enormously popular within and outside Great Britain.

The austere 1950s were succeeded by the "**Swinging Sixties**", a period of cultural upheaval and optimism which saw the rise of youth culture, London become the epicentre of the fashion universe, and, of course, The Beatles.

The decade ended badly in Northern Ireland where violent disputes, known as **The Troubles**, flared up between Protestant and Catholic organisations.

Despite the efforts of the British Army and the Royal Ulster Constabulary, over the next 29 years some 3,700 people were to lose their lives, many in indiscriminate bombings.

## THATCHERISM

By contrast with the upbeat 1960s the 1970s was a decade of industrial slump and strife. Against this background, in 1979, **Margaret Thatcher**, Britain's first ever female party leader (of the Conservatives) also became Britain's first ever female prime minister. She went on to become the most charismatic leader since Winston Churchill but her ideology, which came to be known as **Thatcherism** – deeply in favour of individualism over collectivism and capitalism over social responsibility – polarised the country. The bitter year-long miners' strike of 1984–85 and subsequent pit closures and massive job losses were the most obvious sign of this. Yet while Britain's industrial base declined other sectors of the economy (mostly services) boomed. Thatcher went on to win three general elections and while she was reviled by many, some look back fondly on her strong style of leadership.

## NEW LABOUR

Although Britain had joined the **European (Economic) Union** in 1973, European policy issues had remained mostly on the back burner. In the post-Thatcher years, however, these, alongside other issues like the immensely unpopular poll tax, led to the unravelling of the Conservatives. John Major gave the Tories another term after Thatcher stepped down, but by 1997 the reformed centrist media-savvy Labour party, reborn as New Labour under **Tony Blair**, had taken centre stage. His dynamic, reformist and optimistic brand of politics earned him a massive majority in Parliament, with policies that moved away from traditional labour values in favour of The City, big business and closer links with Europe.

The creation of the Scottish Parliament and the Welsh Assembly, which were both ratified in 1997, marked a new

# Scottish History

## The Romans 1C AD–4C AD

The Roman conquest of Caledonia was never fully accomplished although there were two main periods of occupation. The initial one (c.80–c.100), which started with Julius Agricola's push northwards, is notable for the victory at Mons Graupius (somewhere in the Northeast). The second period followed the death in AD138 of the Emperor Hadrian (builder of the wall). By the end of the 4C Roman power was waning.

## The Dark Ages 4C–11C

The Barbarian invasions forced the indigenous Britons to take refuge in the wilds of Cornwall, Wales, and beyond Hadrian's Wall in southwest Scotland. It was at Whithorn that the Romano-Briton St Ninian established the first Christian community in the late-4C. Over the next centuries, Christianity gained footing.

In the 8C and 9C the first Norse raiders arrived. These were followed by peaceful settlers in search of new lands, who occupied the Western Isles. The kingdoms of the Picts and Scots merged, under the Scot Kenneth MacAlpine, to form Alba, the territory north of the Forth and Clyde which later became known as Scotia, while the western fringes remained under Norse sway. Territorial conflicts with the English and the Norsemen marked the next two centuries.

## Medieval Scotland

Under the influence of Queen Margaret, and during the reigns of her sons – in particular Edgar, Alexander I and David I – the Celtic kingdom took on a feudal character as towns grew and royal charters were granted. Monastic life flourished as religious communities from France set up sister houses throughout Scotland. In 1098 King Edgar, son of Malcolm III (Canmore), ceded the islands to Norway. Alexander II (1214–49) attempted to curb Norse rule but it was his son Alexander III (1249–86) who, following the Battle of Largs, returned the Western Isles to Scotland. Relations with England remained tense.

## Wars of Independence

On the death in 1290 of Alexander III's granddaughter, the direct heir to the throne, Edward I installed John Balliol as king (and his vassal). However, following Balliol's 1295 treaty with the French, Edward set out for the north on the first of several "pacification" campaigns and thus started a long period of intermittent warfare.

The years of struggle for independence from English overlordship helped forge a national identity and heroes. William Wallace led early resistance, achieving a famous victory at Stirling Bridge (1297). However, he was captured in 1305 and taken to London where he was executed. The next to rally opposition was Robert the Bruce (1274–1329), grandson of one of the original Competitors and therefore with a legitimate claim to the throne. Following the killing of John Comyn, the son of another Competitor, and the representative of the Balliol line, Bruce had himself crowned at Scone in 1306. Slowly he forced the submission of the varying fiefs and his victory at Bannockburn (1314) was crucial in achieving independence.

## The Stewarts (Stuarts)

Although now independent, royal authority was undermined by feuds and intrigue as bloody power struggles broke out among the clan chiefs. The monarchy prevailed, however, and the powerful Albany and Douglas clans were subdued in the 15C. The Scots also supported France in its rivalry with England and the first of many "auld alliances" were forged. In 1424 James I took the reins of power. His son James II succeeded in 1437 following the assassination of his father at Perth. In 1460 James II was killed at the siege of Roxburgh Castle and James III became king. In 1513 the accession of James IV followed his father's death at the Battle of Sauchieburn. James IV was also to die in war, at Flodden in 1513. His son James V. died at Falkland Palace in 1542, leaving his queen, Mary of Guise, and their daughter Mary, who assumed the title Queen of Scots. However, when the Scots refused an alliance between the young Mary and Henry VIII's son, Edward,

English troops invaded, in what was known as The Rough Wooing.

Meanwhile a growing French influence at court was resented by the nobility and the Reformation, fired up by John Knox's sermons, gained ground; monastic houses were destroyed and Catholicism was banned. During the short tragic reign (1561–67) of Mary Queen of Scots, conspiracies and violence were rife and personal scandal finally turned the populace to rebellion. Her flight to England, after her abdication in favour of her infant son, ended in imprisonment and execution by Elizabeth I.

### The Stuarts and Commonwealth

James VI united the crowns of Scotland and England under one monarch, following the childless death of his cousin, Elizabeth I of England. In the 17C James VI attempted to achieve control of the Church through bishops appointed by the crown. His son, Charles I, aroused further strong Presbyterian opposition with the forced introduction of the Scottish Prayer Book. In 1638 the National Covenant was drawn up, which pledged defiance of the religious policy of Charles I. In 1644 led by Montrose, the Covenanters were victorious but defeat came at the Battle of Philiphaugh (1645) and Montrose was forced into exile. After the death of Charles I, Cromwell finished off the Covenanters' army.

The death of Charles II – and the prospect of a new line of openly Catholic monarchs with the accession of his brother James VII – inspired the ill-fated Monmouth rebellion led by Charles II's natural son. In 1689 the Protestant Mary and William were invited to rule. Viscount Dundee rallied the Jacobites (those faithful to King James VII) but after an initial victory at Killiecrankie the Highland army was crushed at Dunkeld. In 1707 the Crowns of England and Scotland were joined together in the Act of Union.

### Highland Clearances

The Jacobite uprising of 1745 was led by Charles Edward Stuart, otherwise known as Bonnie Prince Charlie (1720–88). His Highland Army won an initial victory at Prestonpans but he was defeated at Culloden in 1746 and fled into exile. The aftermath was tragic for the Highlands. Highlanders were disarmed, their national dress proscribed and chieftains deprived of their rights. Eviction and loss of the traditional way of life ensued; this period became known as the Highland Clearances and was complete by around 1860. Mass emigration followed for the many who faced abject poverty.

### Industrial Revolution

From around 1790 onwards, Scotland was becoming one of the commercial and industrial powerhouses of the British Empire, with flourishing textile, coal mining, engineering, railway construction and steel industries. Most famously, Glasgow and the Clyde became a major shipbuilding centre and Glasgow became "Second City of the Empire" after London. Up until the First World War fishing was also a major economic activity.

### Post-Second World War

As traditional heavy industries went into decline or moved to other parts of the world, Scotland's economy waned badly. However, in the late-1970s, the discovery and exploitation of North Sea oil and natural gas in the fields around the Shetland Isles proved a massive boon to Scotland in general and to the Highlands and Islands in particular. In the last three decades the economy has moved to a technology and service base, as the oil runs out. Today it is estimated that around 80 percent of all Scotland's employees work in services, a sector which enjoyed signifcant growth until 2008 and the slump of 2009.

### An Independent Voice

Although the Scottish Parliament was abolished in 1707 there had been calls for Scottish devolution, if not quite full independence, since the mid-18C. In 1999 the Scottish Parliament was reinstated, and in 2005 moved to their new permanent residence at the foot of the Royal Mile in Edinburgh. The Parliament has responsibility over wide areas of Scottish affairs, even though in theory at least, Westminster retains powers to amend or even abolish it. A referendum for full Scottish independence is now mooted for 2014 or 2015.

stage in the relationships between the constituent parts of the United Kingdom though most of the real power has remained firmly rooted in Whitehall and Westminster.

The decade ended under a shadow as Tony Blair's reign gave way to the failure of Gordon Brown's premiership, dogged by the continuing wars in **Iraq** and **Afghanistan**, increasing crime, human rights and privacy issues, and the beginning of a serious recession.

**1947** Independence and partition of India. Nationalisation of railways and road transport
**1950–1953** Korean War
**1952** Accession of **Elizabeth II**
**1958** Treaty of Rome - European Economic Community/EEC (now the European Union/EU)
**1959** Discovery of North Sea oil
**1965** Death of Sir Winston Churchill
**1969** Beginning of "**The Troubles**" in Northern Ireland
**1973** United Kingdom becomes a founding member of the EEC
**1979** **Margaret Thatcher** elected first woman Prime Minister (serves until 1991)

**1982** Falklands War
**1990–1991** Gulf War
**1992–1995** Bosnian War
**1997** Election of a **Labour Government**, led by **Tony Blair**.
**1998** Good Friday Agreement, referendum and meeting of Northern Ireland Assembly
**1999** Opening of Scottish Parliament and Welsh Assembly
**2001-present** Afghanistan War
**2002** Queen's Golden Jubilee.
**2003** Iraq War
**2005** Terrorist bombs explode in London killing 52 people
**2007** Gordon Brown becomes the new prime minister
**2008** UK economy enters recession. Troops withdrawn from Iraq.
**2009** Last surviving British soldier of WWI dies.

## COALITION

**2010** - The Labour government are routed but, with no clear majority for the other parties the first coalition government in the UK since the Second World War sees the Conservatives and the Liberal Democats sharing power.

# Art and Culture

## ARCHITECTURE
### ROMAN

Pre-Roman, Iron Age architecture is best observed in impressive hillforts such as at Maidenhead and in Scottish brochs. The Roman invasion began in Kent; **Richborough Castle** was part of the Roman system of coastal defences, a series of forts in the southeast under the control of the "Count of the Saxon Shore". Their capital was St Albans, linked by military roads to other major settlements in Bath, Chester, Lincoln and York. London was a trading post near a river crossing on the Thames.

Examples of domestic Roman architecture in Britain are the theatre at St Albans and the ruined **villas** at Chedworth, Fishbourne, Bignor and Brading with their mosaics. Their greatest military enterprise was **Hadrian's Wall**, a defensive wall reinforced by military camps stretching from Wallsend on the Tyne to Bowness on the Solway Firth (73mi/117km) to guard the northern boundary of the Empire.

## PRE-ROMANESQUE

Few buildings survive from this period, AD c.650 to the Norman Conquest. Much Saxon work, in timber, was destroyed in Viking raids. **All Saints, Brixworth** (c.680) in Northamptonshire makes use of Roman brick and the apse was surrounded by an external ring-crypt, a feature first found in St Peter's in Rome (c.590).

**All Saints**, at **Earl's Barton** nearby, has a late Saxon tower. Saxon crypts survive at **Hexham**, **Repton** and **Ripon**.

## ECCLESIASTICAL ARCHITECTURE

### Saxon towers

EARL'S BARTON, Northamptonshire – Late 10C

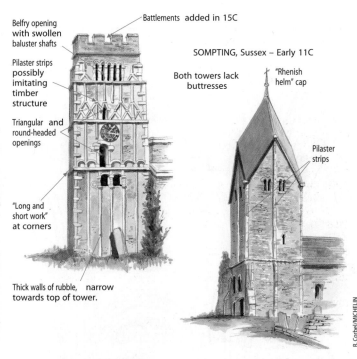

Belfry opening with swollen baluster shafts

Battlements added in 15C

Pilaster strips possibly imitating timber structure

SOMPTING, Sussex – Early 11C

Both towers lack buttresses

"Rhenish helm" cap

Triangular and round-headed openings

Pilaster strips

"Long and short work" at corners

Thick walls of rubble, narrow towards top of tower.

R. Corbel/MICHELIN

## ROMANESQUE (NORMAN)

These bold, massive buildings continued to be erected until after the death of Henry II in 1189 and nowhere else in Europe is there such a richness or variation of Norman work, nor such an abundance of surviving examples. In English cathedrals, the naves tend to be much longer than on the continent, for example **Ely** (13 bays) and **Norwich** (14); the eastern end was usually shorter. **Durham Cathedral**, begun in 1093, where the whole interior is one Romanesque scheme, is a fine example of Norman work in Britain, though externally only the lower parts of the tower and nave and the choir show true Romanesque work. Its stone vaulting, completed in 1133, survives in its original form. **Southwell Minster** has a west front c.1130, with later Perpendicular windows. The eastern end of **Norwich Cathedral** is

tri-apsidal. Its spire and clerestory are later Gothic, but the remainder is Norman. **Rochester**, **Gloucester**, **Peterborough**, **Lincoln**, **Exeter**, **Hereford**, **St Albans**, and the abbey churches of **Tewkesbury** and **Waltham**, are all part of England's heritage of Norman work. Every county boasts many parish churches with a Norman nave or tower, west doorway, or south porch or chancel arch. **Iffley Church**, Oxfordshire, west front (c.1170), **St Mary and St David, Kilpeck**, Herefordshire (c.1140) with Scandinavian influence in the carving, and **St Nicholas, Barfreston**, Kent, are just some of the hundreds well worth visiting. Most secular buildings are fortifications. The **White Tower**, the keep of the Tower of London, was the first work (1080) of William the Conqueror; it had four storeys (over 90ft/30m high), massive walls (over 20ft/6m thick at

### Norman cathedral

Durham Cathedral was largely completed between 1095 and 1133. It exemplifies the grandeur and solidity of Norman architecture. The characteristic rounded arch prevails, but the pointed-rib vaults anticipate the structural achievements of Gothic architecture.

The side elevation of the nave is divided into: triforium/clerestory and arcade

Corbel

Rounded crossing arch

Diagonal ribs

Pointed-rib vault

Blind arcade

Round pier with incised chevrons

Compound pier

Pier with lozenge decoration

Cushion capital

Choir

Nave

19C rood screen

18C rose window

R. Corbel/MICHELIN

## Norman doorway

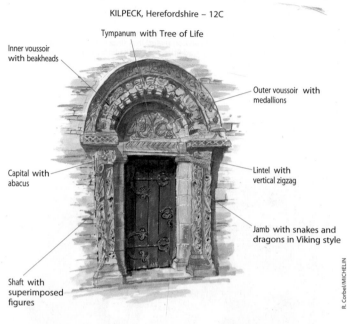

KILPECK, Herefordshire – 12C

Tympanum with Tree of Life

Inner voussoir
with beakheads

Outer voussoir with
medallions

Capital with
abacus

Lintel with
vertical zigzag

Jamb with snakes and
dragons in Viking style

Shaft with
superimposed
figures

R. Corbel/MICHELIN

the base) and small well-protected openings. **Rochester Castle** c.1130, though ruined, gives an impression of living conditions, with passages, garderobes and bedchambers in the thickness (12ft/3.5m) of the walls. **Chepstow Castle** (1067) is one of the earliest secular stone buildings in Britain.

## GOTHIC

The style evolved in northern France; the Abbey of St Denis outside Paris is the earliest example. Gothic designs resulted in larger and higher buildings, flooded with light. Heavy columns were replaced by slimmer clustered column shafts; towers became taller and more slender.

In England Gothic architecture remained in use much longer than elsewhere in Europe, as it evolved through four distinct phases and retained its distinctive English characteristics.

### Transitional (1145–89)

Transitional buildings have both pointed and round arches, especially in windows and vaults. **Ripon Cathedral** (1181) is a good example but the most outstanding is the choir of **Canterbury Cathedral**.

### Early English (c.1190–1307)

Distinctive features are the ribbed vaults, narrow pointed arches and lancet windows. **Salisbury Cathedral**, built, apart from tower and spire, between 1220 and 1258, is the only English cathedral to have been built virtually in one operation, hence in a single style. See also **Wells**, the façades of **Peterborough** and **Ripon**, much of **Lichfield**, and the Abbeys of **Tintern** and **Fountains**, and **Bolton Priory**.

### Decorated (c.1280–1377)

**Ely Cathedral**, with its octagon and lantern (1323–30), was one of the early experiments in new spatial form and lighting. Other examples include the west façades of **Exeter** and **York**.

### Perpendicular

The last – and longest – phase of Gothic architecture in Britain is uniquely English in style. There is an emphasis on vertical lines but the principal features are

## Gothic

### SALISBURY CATHEDRAL (1220-58)

Of great length and highly compartmentalised in layout like most English cathedrals, Salisbury is exceptional in having been completed in a single style – Early English – in a short space of time. The only major addition was the tall crossing tower and spire (404ft) built c 1334.

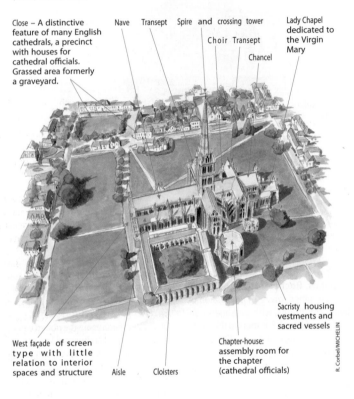

Close – A distinctive feature of many English cathedrals, a precinct with houses for cathedral officials. Grassed area formerly a graveyard.

Nave    Transept    Spire and crossing tower

Choir    Transept

Chancel

Lady Chapel dedicated to the Virgin Mary

West façade of screen type with little relation to interior spaces and structure

Aisle    Cloisters

Chapter-house: assembly room for the chapter (cathedral officials)

Sacristy housing vestments and sacred vessels

R. Corbel/MICHELIN

### WINDOWS

Simple 5-lancet Early English window c 1170, tall, narrow and with acutely-pointed arch

Space between lancets enlivened by addition of quatrefoil c 1270

Window in Decorated style with fully developed flowing tracery c 1350

Large window in Perpendicular style with 4-centred arch and horizontal emphasis through use of transoms

R. Corbel/MICHELIN

## VAULTING

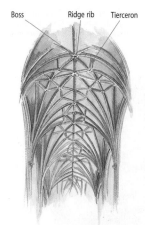

Nave vault with liernes (linking ribs not joined to central boss or springer)
Canterbury Cathedral c 1390 - 1405

Boss  Ridge rib  Tierceron

Fan vault with pendants: the ultimate development of this highly ornamental, non-structural vault
Henry VII's Chapel, Westminster 1503-12

R. Corbel/MICHELIN

panelled decoration all over the building, an increase in window area and the consequent development – very much later than in France – of the flying buttress. Fan-vault roofing, a peculiarly English design, can best be seen in **King's College Chapel**, Cambridge (1146–1515), **Eton College Chapel** (1441) and **St George's Chapel**, Windsor (1475–1509).

Contemporary with the fan vault, and equally English, was the development of the **timber roof**. Tie and collar designs from the 13C and 14C developed into more complex 15C and 16C **hammer-beam** roofs over churches and guild-halls, of which **Westminster Hall** (Hugh Herland, c.1395) is an example. Others are the Great Hall at **Hampton Court** (1535) and **Rufford Old Hall**, near Ormskirk, Lancashire (1505). England also has a wealth of medieval timber-framed houses, built in areas where stone was scarce – **Rufford Old Hall**, the **Guildhall** at Lavenham and the **Feathers Hotel** in Ludlow.

## TUDOR–JACOBEAN

This period began with the accession of Henry VII in 1485 and covers the transition from Gothic to Classicism. Tudor Gothic, both ecclesiastical and secular, can be seen in **Bath Abbey** and the brick-built **Hampton Court Palace**.

From 1550 to 1620 building was largely domestic, for a thriving middle class and a wealthy aristocracy. **Longleat House** (1550–80) in Wiltshire, **Montacute House** (1588–1601) in Somerset, and Bess of Hardwick's **Hardwick Hall** (1591–97) in Derbyshire are outstanding examples. The courtyard layout of medieval days was abandoned for the E- or H-shaped plan, a central rectangular block with projecting wings. The **Long Gallery** – used for exercise on winter days – became a feature of all the great houses of the Elizabethan period.

Half-timbered houses were built in areas where stone was scarce – **Little Moreton Hall** (1559) in Cheshire and **Speke Hall**, near Liverpool, begun in 1490 and still being added to in 1612. The staircase began to assume an importance in the design of Elizabethan houses and by Jacobean times had become, in many houses, the focus of the whole interior – Ham, Hatfield, Knole and Audley End.

The architectural ideas of the **Renaissance** were brought to England by **Inigo Jones** (1573–1652). His two most outstanding public buildings are the **Banqueting Hall** (1619–22) in London and the **Queen's House** (1616–35) in Greenwich.

He also rebuilt part of **Wilton House** (1647–53) in Wiltshire, where his adherence to Classical proportions is

## LITTLE MORETON HALL, Cheshire

A moated manor house built between the mid-15C and c 1580 with elaborate timber-framing and carved decoration characteristic of the Welsh Marches, Cheshire and Lancashire. Despite its date, this, and many other houses like it, is still medieval in character.

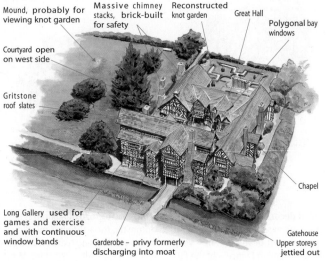

Mound, probably for viewing knot garden

Massive chimney stacks, brick-built for safety

Reconstructed knot garden

Great Hall

Polygonal bay windows

Courtyard open on west side

Gritstone roof slates

Chapel

Long Gallery used for games and exercise and with continuous window bands

Garderobe – privy formerly discharging into moat

Gatehouse Upper storeys jettied out

R. Corbel/MICHELIN

## BLENHEIM PALACE AND PARK, Oxfordshire

Built 1705-22 by Sir John Vanbrugh, the Palace with its vast scale, heroic proportions and rich profusion of forms represents the culmination of the Baroque style in England. The park was transformed between 1764-74 by Lancelot "Capability" Brown, whose masterpiece it is.

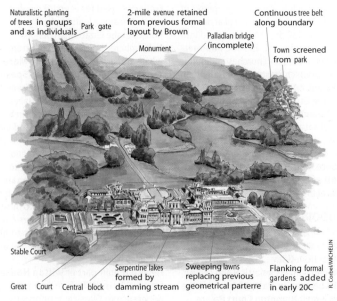

Naturalistic planting of trees in groups and as individuals

Park gate

2-mile avenue retained from previous formal layout by Brown

Monument

Palladian bridge (incomplete)

Continuous tree belt along boundary

Town screened from park

Stable Court

Great  Court  Central block

Serpentine lakes formed by damming stream

Sweeping lawns replacing previous geometrical parterre

Flanking formal gardens added in early 20C

R. Corbel/MICHELIN

## English Baroque

ST PAUL'S CATHEDRAL, City of London, West façade

Built by Sir Christopher Wren between 1675 and 1710, the cathedral combines Renaissance and Baroque elements in a masterly way. The dome, inspired by St Peter's in Rome, is in three parts: the lightweight and beautifully shaped outer dome, an inner dome, and between them an (invisible) brick core carrying the heavy lantern which helps hold the outer dome in place.

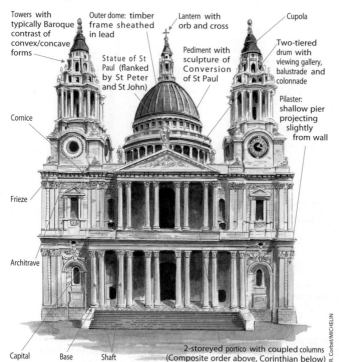

Towers with typically Baroque contrast of convex/concave forms

Outer dome: timber frame sheathed in lead

Lantern with orb and cross

Cupola

Two-tiered drum with viewing gallery, balustrade and colonnade

Statue of St Paul (flanked by St Peter and St John)

Pediment with sculpture of Conversion of St Paul

Pilaster: shallow pier projecting slightly from wall

Cornice

Frieze

Architrave

Capital  Base  Shaft

2-storeyed portico with coupled columns (Composite order above, Corinthian below)

R. Corbel/MICHELIN

evident in the "double cube" room. Architects in England who had never seen an ancient Classical building based their work on "Pattern Books" published by Renaissance designers.

### Tudor Forts

In 1538, faced with the threat of invasion to re-establish the Pope's authority, Henry VIII began to construct a chain of forts and batteries to prevent an enemy invasion fleet from making use of the principal anchorages, landing places and ports.

The first forts built in 1539-40 – Deal, Walmer and Dover in Kent, Calshot and Hurst, overlooking Southampton Water and The Solent, and St Mawes and Pendennis in Cornwall – were squat

with thick walls and rounded parapets. In most a central circular keep was surrounded by lower round bastions or enclosed by a circular curtain wall. They were designed to be defended by cannon mounted on carriages and sited on several tiers of platforms to compensate for the limited vertical traverse of each cannon. Lateral traverse was limited only by the splay of the gun ports.

## CLASSICISM

Though Classicism was introduced by Inigo Jones, it was in the reign of Charles I (1625–49) that the style really began to make its mark on the English scene. The dominant figure was **Sir Christopher Wren** (1632-1723). After the Great Fire of London, he was respon-

## VICTORIAN ARCHITECTURE

### ST PANCRAS STATION, London

The Midland Hotel, completed in the Gothic Revival style in 1876 by Sir George Gilbert Scott, conceals the great train shed whose iron and glass arch was the widest (249ft) in the world at the time. Marrying Venetian, French, Flemish and English Gothic in a triumphal synthesis, Scott's building was also a functional masterpiece, housing the myriad activities of a railway terminus on a restricted, triangular site.

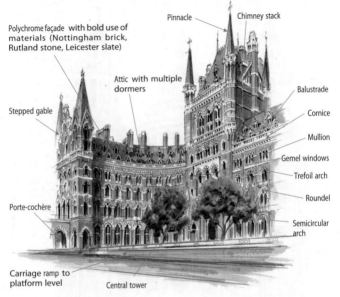

Pinnacle

Chimney stack

Polychrome façade with bold use of materials (Nottingham brick, Rutland stone, Leicester slate)

Attic with multiple dormers

Balustrade

Stepped gable

Cornice

Mullion

Gemel windows

Trefoil arch

Roundel

Porte-cochère

Semicircular arch

Carriage ramp to platform level

Central tower

R. Corbel/MICHELIN

sible for 53 churches and the new **St Paul's Cathedral**, as well as the **Royal Naval College** at Greenwich and a new wing for **Hampton Court Palace**, which harmonises well with the Tudor brickwork. The **Sheldonian Theatre** (1669) at Oxford, and the **Library** of **Trinity College**, Cambridge (1676–84) are two of his best-known works outside London.

**Sir John Vanbrugh** (1664–1726), soldier and playwright, who turned architect in 1699, was one of the chief exponents of the **Baroque** in England; his masterpieces, produced in collaboration with **Nicholas Hawksmoor** (1661–1736), are **Castle Howard**, **Blenheim Palace** and **Seaton Delaval**. Hawksmoor, under a commission of 1711, designed six London churches. **St Mary Woolnoth** in the City of London survives to shows his style.

Baroque architecture brought fantasy and movement to the Classical order but found little favour in England. It was replaced in the 1720s with **Palladianism**, also a foreign "implant" but one with a symmetry which was eagerly adapted by architects such as **Colen Campbell** (**Houghton Hall**) and **William Kent** (**Holkham Hall**). Palladian houses were set carefully in landscaped parks – many by **Lancelot "Capability" Brown** – a far cry from the formality of French and Italian gardens of the period. He designed over 170 parks, remodeling the great estate parks of the English gentry to resemble an ordered version of nature.

**Robert Adam** (1728-92), son of a Scottish architect, returned from the Grand Tour, having absorbed the principles of ancient architecture and learnt much neoclassical theory. He and his brothers set up in practice in London in 1758,

## GEORGIAN HOUSING AND PLANNING

In the 18C and early 19C, extensions to inland spas, and later to seaside towns saw a fusion of urban planning and landscape design. In Bath, John Wood the Elder and John Wood the Younger built the splendidly urbane sequence of Queen Square (1736), Gay Street (1734-60), The Circus (1754) and Royal Crescent, the latter a palace-like composition made up of relatively small terraced houses facing out to parkland.

Royal Crescent

Landsdown Crescent, unusually undulating in plan (1792)

Ha-ha sunken wall permitting uninterrupted view

The Circus    Gay Street

R. Corbel/MICHELIN

In London, strict regulations governed the design of terraced houses which were rated 1-4 according to their size and value.

Sash-windows with thin wooden glazing bars help unify façades. Small or square windows of top floor act as visual stop. Classical appearance aided by low-pitched roofs (sometimes partly concealed by parapet) and lack of emphasis on chimneys. Tall windows emphasize importance of first floor reception rooms.

First-rate house

Second-rate house

Third-rate house

Fourth-rate house

R. Corbel/MICHELIN

introducing a lighter, more decorative style than the Palladian work then in vogue. Most of Adam's buildings are domestic and he also had great flair as an interior designer.

## 19C AND 20C ARCHITECTURE

The 19C was predominantly an age of stylistic revivals. The Industrial Revolution and the movement of people into towns stimulated the construction of factories and mills and housing. Iron and glass played a part in the mass-production of these buildings. At first individual craftsmanship was evident in mouldings, decoration and furniture but by 1900 much of this had vanished.

**John Nash** (1752–1835), builder of many terraces round Regent's Park and down Regent Street in London, also designed the **Royal Pavilion** at Brighton. **Sir John Soane** (1753–1837), probably the last of the original designers, is represented by his house at Lincoln's Inn Fields, now the **Sir John Soane Museum.**

From 1840 the trend was towards the Gothic Revival which reached its height between 1855 and 1885. **Sir Charles Barry** (1795–1860) rebuilt the **Palace of Westminster** after the 1834 fire. Alfred Waterhouse (1830–1905) designed the Natural History Museum and built Manchester Town Hall.

The 19C was also the Railway Age. **Isambard Kingdom Brunel** (1806–59), Chief Engineer to the Great Western Railway in 1833, also designed the Clifton Suspension Bridge. **Thomas Telford** (1757–1834) built roads, bridges and canals throughout the country. He was responsible for the London–Holyhead road and for the bridge (1826), which carries it over the Menai Strait. In the 20C Art Nouveau had little influence on architecture but there was passing interest in interior decoration, fabrics and stained glass in the new style. Reinforced concrete was the main structural development.

Between the wars, the outstanding figure was **Sir Edwin Lutyens** (1869–1944), who adapted Classicism to the needs of the day, in civic and housing design as well as ecclesiastical. His was the genius behind New Delhi in India

and he also designed the **Cenotaph** in Whitehall and **Hampstead Garden Suburb** in London. **Sir Giles Gilbert Scott** (1880–1960), grandson of Sir George, the 19C architect, built the last great cathedral in the Gothic style, the red sandstone **Anglican Cathedral** of Liverpool. He also set the pattern for power stations with his 1929 design for **Battersea Power Station**.

"Urban planning" was not a 20C idea. Haussmann redesigned much of Paris in the 1860s and the Italian Renaissance painter Martini has left us his picture, painted in 1475, of *The Ideal City*. In Britain, **Welwyn Garden City**, built near St Albans in 1920, was one of the first New Towns, an extension of the Garden Suburb concept. The planned layout of streets, cul-de-sacs and closes, romantically named and lined with semi-detached and detached houses, was copied across the country after the 1939–45 war, in an attempt to check the "urban sprawl" in London, Lancashire, the Clyde Valley and South Wales. The 1946 New Towns Act provided for 28 such New Towns; **Harlow New Town** by Gibberd was built in 1947, **Cumbernauld**, near Glasgow, in the 1950s and **Milton Keynes** in rural Buckinghamshire in the 1970s. As costs escalated and concern grew over the decay of city centres, the building of new towns was halted. Pedestrian zones and the banishing of traffic have helped to conserve both the fabric and spirit of established town and city centres. **Poundbury** village in Dorchester, Dorset (1993–94), which stresses the importance of architecture on a human scale and is sponsored by the Prince of Wales, represents the latest trend in urban planning.

Outstanding among examples of 20C architecture is Sir Basil Spence's **Coventry Cathedral** (1956–62), remarkable in itself and in the way it blends with the older buildings around it. The imaginative circular design of **Liverpool Metropolitan Cathedral** (consecrated 1967) was the work of **Sir Frederick Gibberd**. In the secular sphere, education – established and new universities – and the arts provided good opportunities for pioneering work: Sainsbury Centre for Visual Arts, East Anglia, Norman Foster 1991; Downing College library, Cambridge, Quinlan Terry 1987; St John College Garden Quad, Oxford, 1993.

Custom-built galleries were designed for the Sainsbury Collection (1970s) at Norwich (Norman Foster), Burrell's donation in Glasgow (B Gasson) and the Tate Gallery at St Ives (1993, Evans and Shalev).

Other areas which have provided great scope for exciting modern architecture over the last few years are sports venues – the new **Wembley Stadium** and Lord's Cricket Ground stand (Michael Hopkins); opera houses – Glyndebourne and Covent Garden, **Royal Opera House** refurbishment and extension; London office developments – **Lloyd's Building**, Canary Wharf, Broadgate, The Ark, Swiss Re Tower ("**The Gherkin**") and City Hall. Major commissions (bridges, community and other projects) approved by the Millennium Commission heralded an explosion of original design for the turn of the century. Many of these are now popular visitor attractions: the **Eden Project**, Cornwall; Dynamic Earth, Edinburgh; the Great Glass-

The Swiss Re Building – the "Gherkin", City of London

VisitLondonImages/Pawel Libera

house at the National Botanic Garden of Wales; in Manchester, The Lowry, The Imperial War Museum of the North and Urbis; in Glasgow, the Glasgow Science Centre and **The Armadillo**. All break new ground in structural and materials technology.

The most controversial projects have been the reviled **Millennium Dome**, London, and the **Scottish Parliament building** in Edinburgh.

The Parliament building was finally completed in 2004, three years late and ten times over-budget. The Dome was a commercial failure for many years and

## EARLY MODERN ARCHITECTURE

### GLASGOW SCHOOL OF ART

In touch with continental Art Nouveau and looking forward to 20C functionalism, Charles Rennie Mackintosh was also inspired by the robust forms of Scottish baronial architecture. Rising castle-like from its steeply sloping site, his Glasgow School of Art (1897-1909) combines strict utility of purpose with innovative, near-abstract forms and decorative Art Nouveau elements.

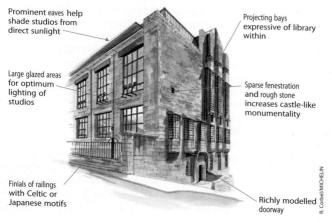

Prominent eaves help shade studios from direct sunlight

Projecting bays expressive of library within

Large glazed areas for optimum lighting of studios

Sparse fenestration and rough stone increases castle-like monumentality

Finials of railings with Celtic or Japanese motifs

Richly modelled doorway

R. Corbel/MICHELIN

only recently (under its new guise as the O2 Arena) has found great success as a concert venue.

The regeneration of derelict industrial sites and obsolete docks has met with considerable success in Liverpool, Cardiff and particularly the massive **London Dockland** scheme of the 1990s (still ongoing).

The conservation and reuse of existing industrial buildings is most apparent in two huge and stunning art galleries at opposite ends of the country: **Tate Modern**; in London (formerly a power station): the **Baltic Centre for Contemporary Art**, in Gateshead (formerly a flour mill).

## PARKS AND GARDENS

A keen appreciation of country life and the pleasures of nature goes back to the Middle Ages when Royal Forests covered much of the land and every person of consequence had a deer park. It was in the 18C, however, that the face of lowland Britain was transformed in pursuit of the aesthetic ideals of the country's "greatest original contribution to the arts", the **English Landscape Movement**. Ruthlessly sweeping away the grand avenues, parterres and topiary of the previous century, the grandees and lesser gentry of the Georgian age, aided by professionals like **Lancelot "Capability" Brown** (1716–83) and **Humphry Repton** (1752–1818), swept away the boundaries separating house, garden and surrounding countryside to make ambitious compositions fusing buildings and statuary, lawns and woodland, lakes and rivers into a picturesque vision of idealised nature. The movement embraced the Ideal Theory of Art, where everyday objects were seen as imperfect copies of universal ideas, for the artist to perfect. As well as their grander creations (**Blenheim**, Stourhead), there are many lesser achievements in the field of landscape beautification, which has bequeathed a national passion for landscaping and horticulture.

Britain has a wonderful heritage of gardens, many of which are open to visitors. Owing to the vagaries of the climate, particularly the closeness of the Gulf Stream, conditions have proved favourable to many of the plant collections brought back from all over the world, particularly in the 18C and 19C. The chief name in garden design in the late-19C and early-20C was Gertrude Jekyll (Knebworth and Broughton Castle), who often worked in collaboration with the architect Sir Edwin Lutyens.

Plant trials and serious **horticultural study** are conducted at **Kew Gardens** in London, at **Wisley** in Surrey, the gardens of the Royal Horticultural Society, at Harlow Carr and the Botanic Gardens in Edinburgh (17C) and Glasgow. A few of the earliest **medicinal gardens** are still in existence, such as the Botanic Gardens (1621) in Oxford and the Chelsea Physic Garden (1673) in London.

A Museum of **Garden History** occupies Lambeth parish church and graveyard, where John Tradescant, gardener to King Charles I, is buried. Examples of the early knot garden have been created here and at Hampton Court. Formal gardens with geometric layout can be seen at **Hampton Court**, Ham House and Pitmedden.

The most prevalent style is the famous English Landscape, promoted by Capability Brown and Humphry Repton – **Stourhead** and **Castle Howard**.

The art of **topiary** is practised at Levens Hall and Earlshall in Scotland. The vogue for follies, usually an artificial ruin at the end of a vista, produced **Studley Royal**, which achieves its climax with a view of the ruins of Fountains Abbey.

Less contrived gardens incorporate the natural features of the site, such as **Glendurgan**, which occupies a deep combe on the Cornish coast.

Gardens range from the most southerly, Tresco **Abbey Gardens** in the Scilly Isles, created and maintained since 1834 by successive generations of the same family, to the most northerly, **Inverewe** in Wester Ross, where, despite the northern latitude, the gardens are frost-free, owing to the warm North Atlantic Drift. Sissinghurst and Crathes Castle are examples of themed gardens, where the different enclosures are distinguished by colour, season or plant species.

## VERNACULAR ARCHITECTURE

### CRUCK COTTAGE, HEREFORDSHIRE
Late medieval

The simplest form of timber construction, using the two halves of a massive, curving branch or tree-trunk

### HOUSE AT CULROSS, SCOTLAND 16C

Crow-stepped gable

Rubble walls covered in rough cast ("harling") and colour-washed

### WEALDEN HOUSE, KENT c 1500

Upper floor jettied out

Hipped roof, originally thatched, now tiled

Close-studded vertical timbers

Smoke vent, later replaced by chimney stack

### TIMBER-FRAMED HOUSE, Kent 17C

Timber frame clad in contrasting materials: upper floor with hung tiles, ground floor in weather-boarding

### STONE COTTAGES, Gloucestershire

Built of oolithic limestone, possibly as a 14C monastic sheephouse and converted into cottages in 17C

Steep-pitched roof with graded stone slates

### SEMI-DETACHED SUBURBAN HOUSES
Urban outskirts anywhere in Britain c 1930

Picturesque Arts and Crafts outline and detail. Contrasting treatment: pebble-dash on left, applied "half-timbering" on right

R. Corbel/MICHELIN

## VERNACULAR ARCHITECTURE

From the end of the medieval period, relative peace meant that security was no longer paramount and the fortified castle gave way to the rural residence designed as a setting for artistic patronage, culture, the social round, field sports and farm management; each generation of the rich and powerful seeking to establish or consolidate its status by building or rebuilding in accord with architectural fashion.

It is, however, the everyday architecture of cottage, farmhouse and barn that expresses most strongly the individuality of particular places. The range of materials used is enormous. Every type of stone has been quarried and shaped, from the most intractable of Scottish and Cornish granites to the crumbling chalk of the south. Limestones are often exploited to wonderful effect, as in the **Cotswolds** or the **Yorkshire Wolds**. Where stone is lacking, timber is used as in the **cruck-built cottages** of Herefordshire and the elaborate half-timbered houses of much of the Midlands, or as "**weather-boarding**" cladding in the Southeast. In the claylands, most villages once had their own brickfield, producing distinctive tiles as well as bricks, while reedbeds provided thatch for roofing.

Building forms vary too: from the solid **timber frame** of a Kentish Tudor house to the humble one-roomed dwelling of a crofter in northwest Scotland.

Settlement patterns are also almost infinitely varied: a few cottages and farms may be loosely grouped to form a hamlet; elsewhere, true villages may predominate, street villages accompanying a road for part of its way, others clustering sociably around the green.

## Architectural Terms

**Aisle** – lateral divisions running parallel with the nave in medieval churches and other buildings.

**Ambulatory** – passage between the choir and apse of a church.

**Apse** – rounded or polygonal end of a church.

**Arcade** – a series of arches, resting on piers or columns.

**Architrave** – the beam, or lowest portion of the entablature, extending from column to column. Also used as the moulded frame around the head and side of a window or door opening.

**Baldachin** – canopy supported by pillars set over an altar, throne or tomb.

**Baptistery** – building, separate from the church, containing the font.

**Barbican** – outwork of a medieval castle, often with a tower, defending a gate or bridge.

**Barrel vaulting** – continuous arched vault of semicircular section.

**Battlements** – parapet of medieval fortifications, with a walkway for archers or crossbowmen.

**Broach spire** – octagonal spire rising from a square tower without parapets.

**Buttress** – vertical mass of masonry built against a wall, so strengthening it and resisting the outward pressure of a vaulted roof.

**Capital** – crowning feature of a column or pillar.

**Chancel** – part of the church set aside for clergy and choir, to the east of the nave.

**Chantry chapel** – chapel endowed for religious services for the soul of the founder.

**Chapter house** – place of assembly for the governing body of a monastery or cathedral. In medieval England, often multi-sided, with vaulting supported on a central pillar.

**Chevron** – Norman decoration of zigzag mouldings used around windows and doorways.

**Choir** – western part of the chancel, used by the choir, immediately east of the screen separating nave and chancel.

**Clerestory** – upper storey of the nave of a church, generally pierced by a row of windows.

**Corbel** – stone bracket, often richly carved, projecting from a wall to support roof beams, the ribs of a vault, a statue or an oriel window.

**Cornice** – crowning projection, the upper part of the entablature in Classical architecture. Also used for the projecting decoration around the ceiling of a room.

**Crossing** – central area of a cruciform church, where the transepts cross the nave and choir. A tower is often set above this space.

**Crypt** – underground chamber beneath a church, used as place of burial or charnel-houses. They often also housed the bones or relics of a saint or martyr.

**Cupola** – hemispherical roof.

**Drum** – vertical walling supporting a dome, sometimes with windows.

**Embrasure** – the space between two merlons, on a battlement, through which archers could fire, whil protected by the merlons.

**Entablature** – in Classical architecture, the entire portion above the columns, comprising architrave, frieze and cornice.

**Fan vaulting** – system of vaulting peculiar to English Perpendicular architecture, all ribs having the same curve, resembling the framework of a fan.

**Finial** – top or finishing portion of a pinnacle, gable, bench end or other feature.

**Fluting** – narrow concave channelling cut vertically on a shaft or column.

**Flying buttress** – external arch springing over the roof of an aisle and supporting the clerestory wall, counteracting the thrust of the nave vault.

**Frieze** – central division of the entablature – horizontal decorative design at high level.

**Gable** – triangular end section of a wall of a building, enclosed by the line of the roof.

**Hammerbeam roof** – late Gothic form of roof construction with no tie-beam. Wooden arches rest on corbels and beams bracketed to the walls and eaves.

**Harling** – wall plastered with roughcast. Often painted or with colour incorporated.

**Jamb** – upright side of a window or door opening.

**Keep** – inner tower and strongest part of a medieval fortress.

**Keystone** – central, wedge-shaped stone which locks an arch together.

**Lancet** – Early English (13C) sharp-pointed arch.

**Lantern** – glazed construction, for ventilation and light, often surmounting a dome.

**Lierne** – short intermediate rib in Gothic vaulting.

**Loggia** – open-sided gallery or arcade.

**Machicolation** – in medieval military architecture, a row of openings below a projecting parapet through which missiles could be rained down on the enemy.

**Misericord** – tip-up seat in choir stalls, with a small projection on the underside, to support a person having to stand through a long service. Often fancifully and grotesquely carved.

**Mullions** – vertical ribs dividing a window into a number of lights.

**Narthex** – western portico at the entrance to early Christian churches.

**Nave** – central main body of a church, west of the choir, into which lay persons were admitted, chancel and choir being reserved for the priests.

**Ogee** – arch used in late Gothic period, combining convex and concave curve, ending in a point.

**Oriel** – window projecting from a wall on corbels.

**Pediment** – triangular termination above the entablature, in Classical architecture sometimes "broken" in Renaissance designs.

**Pilaster** – rectangular pillar, projecting from the wall.

**Rose window** – circular window with mullions converging like the spokes of a wheel.

**Screen** – partition, often richly carved, separating nave from choir and chancel.

**Spandrel** – triangular space between the curves of arches and the frame in which they are set.

**Squinch** – arch placed diagonally across the internal corner angles of a square tower, converting the square into an octagonal form.

**Tierceron** – secondary rib in Gothic vaulting.

**Transept** – arms of a cruciform church set at right angles to nave and choir.

**Transom** – horizontal cross-bar or division of a window.

**Tympanum** – space between the flat lintel and the arch of a doorway.

**Undercroft** – vaulted chamber partly or wholly below ground, in a medieval building.

**Volute** – spiral scroll used at the corners of Ionic, Corinthian and Composite capitals.

## SCULPTURE

The idea of erecting statues, in stone and bronze, introduced largely by the Romans, fell into disuse in Britain in the Dark Ages. Gradually, however, pagan influences and Celtic scroll-work were put to Christian service, in standing crosses and in church decoration. Massive carving in Norman churches gave way to glorious tracery, windows, ribs and vaults in Early English and Perpendicular churches and cathedrals, complemented by carved wooden misericords, bench ends, altar screens and font covers. Impressive statuary such as that on the west front of Wells Cathedral has survived Reformation and Puritan depredations, to give an idea of the skills of early craftsmen.

Until the early-18C, statuary tended to be confined to tombs and memorials. The fashion for portrait busts was introduced by those who made the "Grand Tour" of Europe.

First Classical and then Baroque memorials began to grace both cathedrals and churches in the flowering of British sculpture which took place between 1720 and 1840. In the Victorian age in many towns and cities statues were erected to the memory of industrialists and benefactors, municipal worthies and military heroes. There are also some very fine sculpted memorials executed in commemoration of those who died in battle. In the 20C British sculpture has been enlivened by the sometimes controversial works of **Jacob Epstein** and also of **Henry Moore**, whose technique of "natural carving" allowed the grain and shape of the material to dictate the final form. **Barbara Hepworth**, who settled in St Ives in 1943, **Reg Butler** and **Kenneth Armitage** are among other famous modern sculptors.

Monumental sculptures by Jacob Epstein, Eric Gill, Frank Dobson, Henry Moore, Barbara Hepworth and Eduardo Paolozzi among others set the standard for public art in cities, by the sea and in the countryside. Spectacular modern schemes – Broadgate in London, Herne Bay Sculpture Park, Brighton seafront, sculpture at Goodwood near Chichester, Stour Valley Art Project, Yorkshire Sculpture Park, the Gateshead Riverside Sculpture Park, the Northern Arts Project, Glenrothes in Scotland – have inspired major artists to create large-scale outdoor sculptures and promote interest in art in a wider public.

On the contemporary scene the trend is a break with the past as many artists (Damien Hirst, Anish Kapoor, Richard Deacon, Cornelia Parker, Tracey Emin, Alison Wilding, Stephen Hughes, Tony Cragg, Rachel Whiteread among others) invent new idioms which are often provocative. **The Turner Prize** awarded by the Tate Gallery is always controversial even though "installations" which challenge the viewer's preconceptions are increasingly popular.

## PAINTING
### Early Art

The Celtic peoples loved rhythm and curvilinear scroll patterns, which they used in jewellery and later in manuscripts. The Romans brought their wall paintings and mosaics and both later inspired the didactic medieval church murals, which are some of Britain's earliest paintings. Surviving painting from the Saxon and medieval periods consists largely of exquisite work on illuminated manuscripts, such as the **Lindisfarne Gospels** from Holy Island, though the drawings of **Matthew Paris** are notable departures from this stylised work. One of the earliest surviving English paintings is the **Wilton Diptych** (c.1400), now in the National Gallery.

### 16C–8C

British artists never enjoyed that scale of patronage given to European artists by absolute monarchs and the Papacy. Much early portraiture, other than the **Holbein** pictures of Henry VIII and his court, tend to be flat and stiff but the art of the miniature flourished at the court of Elizabeth, where **Nicholas Hilliard** and **Isaac Oliver** created their masterpieces, capturing both the likeness and something of the spirit of the sitters.

The Dutchman **Sir Anthony van Dyck**, knighted by Charles I, enjoyed his

*Detail of Marriage A-la-Mode: 1, The Marriage Settlement (c.1743) by William Hogarth, The National Gallery*

Photo Art Media/HIP/Scala, Florence

patronage and was the first to record the atmosphere of the Stuart Court, in full-size paintings, before the Civil War. Canaletto, a Venetian, enjoyed some aristocratic support in the 1740s, as did **Sir Peter Lely** and **Godfrey Kneller**, both of German origin, who worked in England for long enough to be considered founders of the English portrait painting school. **William Hogarth**, English born and bred, famous for his vivid commentaries on the life of his day, started the idea of public exhibitions of painting, leading ultimately to the founding in 1768 of the **Royal Academy**. **Sir Joshua Reynolds**, its first president, and his contemporary, **Thomas Gainsborough**, raised the status of English painting, especially portraiture, though it was still much influenced by Dutch and Italian example. **Richard Wilson**, a founder of the Royal Academy, was much inspired by the French masters, Claude and Poussin, and founded the English school of **landscape painting**, a fashion which developed in England and spread to include marine scenes as well as country houses and estates.

## 19C TRENDS

The visionary **William Blake** heralded the dawn of English Romanticism. Portraiture by **Sir Thomas Lawrence** and the works of **Sir Henry Raeburn** in Scotland added **Romanticism** to the traditions of Reynolds.

**John Crome** founded the Norwich School in 1803, a regional treatment of landscape painting which was uniquely English. It was continued after his death by **John Sell Cotman**. **John Constable** and **Joseph M W Turner** carried this tradition and its studies of the effects of ever-changing light into the 19C. From 1840 to 1850 **Dante Gabriel Rossetti's** group, the **Pre-Raphaelites** and **Sir Edward Burne-Jones**, made a short-lived return to primitive values and religious and moral subjects. Their designs inspired Art Nouveau, best expressed in England by the work of **William Morris** and **Aubrey Beardsley**.

**Alfred Sisley**, born in Paris of English parents, was an Impressionist whose sense of colour and tone owed much to the founder of the movement, Claude Monet, with whom he painted *en plein air* in France. The **Camden Town Group**, around **Walter Sickert**, returned to the realism of the Post-Impressionists, whose work **Roger Fry** had exhibited in 1911 and the next 20 years saw many short-lived and loose "movements" such as the **Bloomsbury Group**. **Augustus John** was known for his fashionable portraits in an almost Impressionist style.

## 20C

Post-war artists include **Paul Nash** (landscapes infused with symbolism); **Graham Sutherland**, painter of religious themes, landscapes and portraits; and **Sir Stanley Spencer**, who painted biblical scenes in familiar British settings.

In the 1950s **Ben Nicholson** was the major abstract artist. The optimistic 1960s brought Pop Art: **Peter Blake**, **David Hockney**, **Bridget Riley** ("Op Art"). The portraits and figures of **Francis Bacon** and **Lucian Freud** show a darker, more pessimistic outlook.

Contemporary artists who have won acclaim include Gilbert and George, Paula Rego, Beryl Cooke, Ken Currie, Adrian Wizniewski, Stephen Conroy, Peter Howson, Lisa Milroy, Richard Wentworth, Julian Opie, **Damien Hirst** among others.

The Goldsmith College of Art and the Glasgow School of Art are two of the well-known educational establishments which nurture young talent.

Hirst himself was partially responsible for founding The Young British Art group (Angela Bulloch, Michael Landy, Gary Hume, etc.), the country's most recent art phenomenon. Their work is still championed by the Saatchi Gallery, though many YBAs have now been assimilated into the mainstream.

## MUSIC
### FROM POLYPHONY TO INSTRUMENTAL COMPOSITION

As with painting and sculpture, early and medieval English music was largely inspired by religion. The **Chapel Royal** – an institution, not a building – has fostered English music since 1135. **Thomas Tallis** (c.1505–85), organist at Waltham Abbey near London (until it was dissolved) and later at Queen Elizabeth's Chapel Royal, can be credited with beginning the particularly rich tradition of **church music** for which England is famous. He arranged the harmony for the plainsong responses of Merbecke's English church service (Festal Responses in four and five parts), which are still widely in use and also arranged a setting of the Canticles in Dorian Mode and composed numerous anthems, Latin mass settings, lamentations and motets, of which his most famous is the magnificent *Spem in Alium* for forty voices, and of course his equally famous Canon (c.1567). Together with **William Byrd** (1542/3–1623), himself a prolific composer of high-quality church music with whom Tallis was joint organist at the Chapel Royal, he was granted a monopoly on music printing in England (1575).

By the early 17C, **madrigals**, originally an Italian form, with amorous or satirical themes, were being produced in large numbers by English composers, such as Byrd and **John Dowland** (1562–1626), a talented lute player. Folk music dating back much further accompanied the country dance, which survives today as the **Morris Dance**. Composers such as Byrd and **Thomas Morley** (1557–1602), who wrote settings for several of Shakespeare's plays, spread music into the theatre. **John Bull** (1562–1628), a skilled performer and composer for the virginals, ranks for many as one of the founders of the English keyboard repertoire. He is also sometimes linked with the original tune for *God Save the Queen*. **Ben Jonson** (1573–1637) and **Henry Lawes** (1596–1662) among others were leading exponents of the **masque**, which became popular in the 17C, combining music, dance and pageantry.

**Orlando Gibbons** (1583–1625), organist of the Chapel Royal under James I and one of the finest keyboard players of his day, wrote quantities of superb church music, madrigals and music for viols and virginals. **Henry Purcell** (1659–95), considered the greatest British composer of his generation (and by some of all time), wrote much splendid church music, stage music (opera *Dido and Æneas*), music for State occasions and harpsichord and chamber music.

### MUSIC APPLIED TO DRAMA

**Chamber music** (music not intended for church, theatre or public concert room) truly came into its own in the 18C, which also saw great strides taken in the development of English **opera** and the emergence of a new form, the **oratorio**, under the German-English composer **George Frideric Handel** (1685–1759), perhaps its greatest exponent. His vast output included more than 40 operas, 20 or so oratorios, cantatas, sacred music, and numerous orchestral, choral and instrumental works. In 1719–28 the **Royal Academy of Music** was founded as an operatic organisation linked with Handel. The following century (1822) it became an educational institution, later to be joined by the Royal College of Music (1883) and the Royal School of Church Music (1927).

## POST-ROMANTICISM AND THE MODERN AGE

The composer Thomas Arne (1710–78) set to music the words of James Thomson, *Rule Britannia*, in a masque for Alfred, Prince of Wales in 1740. The late-18C to early-19C was rather a fallow period for Britain in terms of musical composition, although the Romantic movement that swept through Europe made itself felt in other arts such as literature (Wordsworth, Coleridge, Scott), and Romantic song cycles were fashionable with the British public in the 19C.

The next British composer of note was **Sir Edward Elgar** (1857–1934), the first to win international acclaim in almost 200 years. His love of the English countryside (he lived near the Malvern Hills) shaped his music, which is infused with an Englishness that captures the spirit of a nation in its heyday as a world power. Works such as *The Enigma Variations* and *The Dream of Gerontius* placed him on the world stage, and his many orchestral works exhibit the composer's masterly orchestration (Symphonies in A flat and E flat, Cello Concerto). **Frederick Delius** (1862–1934), championed by the conductor Sir Thomas Beecham, composed orchestral variations, rhapsodies, concerti and a variety of other orchestral and choral works stamped with his very individual, chromatic approach to harmony. The compositions of **Ralph Vaughan Williams** (1872–1958) were influenced by his study of English folk songs and Tudor church music; throughout his

life he took an active interest in popular movements in music. **Gustav Holst** (1874–1934), prevented from becoming a concert pianist by neuritis in his hand, studied music at the Royal College of Music under Sir Charles Villiers Stanford (1852–1924), an Irish composer of church music and choral works. Holst, an ardent socialist, influenced by his love of the works of Grieg and Wagner as well as a certain innate mysticism, produced his most famous work, the seven-movement orchestral suite *The Planets*, in 1914–16.

**Sir William Walton** (1902–83) rose to fame with his instrumental settings of poems by Edith Sitwell (*Façade*, 1923) and went on to compose symphonies, concerti, opera, the biblical cantata *Belshazzar's Feast* and film music (Laurence Olivier's *Henry V*, *Hamlet* and *Richard III*). **Sir Michael Tippett** (1905–98) won recognition with his oratorio *A Child of Our Time*, reflecting the unrest of the 1930s and 40s, and went on to produce a rich and varied output, including operas *(The Midsummer Marriage, King Priam)*, symphonies and other orchestral works in which he exhibits formidable powers of imagination and invention, combining inspiration from earlier sources such as Purcell with his interest in popular modern music such as blues and jazz.

**Sir Benjamin Britten** (1913–76) studied under John Ireland (1879–1962) at the Royal College of Music and after a couple of years in the USA returned to England where he produced mainly vocal or choral works (one exception being his *Variations and Fugue on a Theme of Purcell*, or *Young Person's Guide to the Orchestra*), notably the operas *Peter Grimes*, *Billy Budd* and *A Midsummer Night's Dream*, *A Ceremony of Carols* and the immensely moving *War Requiem*. **John Tavener** (b.1944), whose haunting *Song for Athene* ended the funeral service of Diana, Princess of Wales, at Westminster Abbey in September 1997, draws the inspiration for his predominantly religious music from his Russian Orthodox faith.

Still popular since their inception by **Sir Henry Wood** (1869–1944) in 1895

81

are the **Promenade Concerts**, which are held at the Royal Albert Hall every summer (mid-July–mid-September). The chorus *Jerusalem* sung as an unofficial anthem at the end of each season of Promenade concerts is perhaps the best-known work of Sir Hubert Parry (1848–1918). Conductors and composers such as Sir Peter Maxwell Davies, Sir Neville Mariner, Sir John Eliot Gardner, Sir Colin Davis, Sir Simon Rattle, Christopher Hogwood and Andrew Davies ensure the continuation of healthy and creative British music.

Eisteddfods in Wales and Mods in Scotland carry on a tradition of the Celtic bards. Festivals, such as the **Three Choirs** at Hereford, Worcester and Gloucester cathedrals and – in completely different spheres – opera productions at **Glyndebourne** and the **English National Opera** contribute to the aim of maintaining public interest in live classical music. However, Glyndebourne remains the reserve of the rich, while opera is usually targeted at the wealthy middle and upper classes.

## CODA

On a lighter note, the meeting in 1875 of **Sir William Gilbert** (1836–1911) and **Sir Arthur Sullivan** (1842–1900) produced an enduring and well-loved English musical tradition in the form of "Gilbert and Sullivan" operas, staged by Richard D'Oyly Carte. **Musical comedy**, an English development of the European operetta, was born in the 1890s at the Gaiety Theatre in London, with shows like *The Gaiety Girl*.

Another typically British institution, the **music hall**, also became popular – variety entertainment with the audience being able to eat and drink while watching the performance. Two names, **Ivor Novello** (1893–1951) and **Sir Noël Coward** (1899–1973), will always be associated with British musical comedy between the world wars. The tradition of British musicals has since been continued most notably by **Sir Andrew Lloyd Webber** (b.1948).

## POP AND ROCK

British pop music began in the 1950s with early pioneers being **Lonnie Donegan** with his skiffle sound and a very youthful **Cliff Richard** doing his best to be the British Elvis Presley. It was **The Beatles**, however, who did more than any band to bring the new genre of "popular music" to the fore. Their first chart hit was in 1962 and they broke up in 1970. During that short but explosive period of creativity, they spawned a whole "Liverpool Sound". Their influence, not only on British but also on world pop and rock music, was incalculable, and reverberates around concert halls and in recording studios even today. **The Beatles**' most famous contemporaries are the equally iconic **Rolling Stones** (from London), still touring and recording today. The 1960s closed to the sound of **Black Sabbath**, **Deep Purple** and **Led Zeppelin** – heavyweights, who were to rule the burgeoning rock music scene for much of the decade until the advent of punk rock in 1977, led most (in)famously by the **Sex Pistols**. The 1980s saw the dance and club scene take off and the rise of Manchester bands such as **The Smiths**, **Stone Roses** and **Happy Mondays**. The decade is best remembered for its frothy pop and pop-soul sounds, however, typified by **Wham** (featuring George Michael), **Culture Club** (Boy George) and **Simply Red**. The 1990s was the era of Britpop, most famously **Blur** and **Oasis**; both quintessentially English bands drawing heavily on 1960s influences. It was also the decade of "boy bands" (**Take That**, **Westlife**, **Blue**) and "girl bands" (**The Spice Girls**, **All Saints**), a vocals-only genre which continues to defy critical disdain and sells millions of albums well into the 21C. Since 2000 television talent shows such as *Pop Idol* and *The X Factor* have "manufactured" Britain's cheesiest pop stars such as **Will Young**, **Gareth Gates** and **Leona Lewis**. Bands such as **Coldplay** and **Radiohead** maintain mainstream British rock. **Dizzee Rascal** leads the local hip-hop and "grime" scene, while **Robbie Williams** and **Pete Doherty** are tabloid rehab favourites.

## LITERATURE
## MIDDLE AGES

**Geoffrey Chaucer** (c.1340–1400), the first great English poet, was influential in the evolution of "standard" English from cruder medieval dialects. The language of the *Canterbury Tales* is consequently as recognisable to us today as are Chaucer's vividly etched characters. **William Langland** (c1330–1400) in the *Vision of Piers Plowman*, and **Sir Thomas Malory** (d. 471) in *Le Morte D'Arthur* also brought a new depth and expressiveness to literature.

## THE ENGLISH RENAISSANCE AND THE ELIZABETHAN AGE

The sonnet was introduced and blank verse became the regular measure of English dramatic and epic poetry. The supreme achievement of this dynamic, expansive period was in the theatre. Ambitious dramatic forms developed by the fiery **Christopher Marlowe** (1564–94) were perfected by the genius of **William Shakespeare** (1564–1616), the greatest dramatist and poet of this or any age. His monumental 37 plays appealed to all classes. **Ben Jonson** (1572–1637) created the English comedy of humours.

## 17C

**John Donne** (1572–1631), courtier, soldier and latterly Dean of St Paul's, was the most important of the Metaphysical poets whose "witty conceits" were concerned with the interaction between soul and body, sensuality and spirit. **John Milton** (1608–74), after Shakespeare arguably England's greatest poet, was also a powerful pamphleteer for the Puritan cause. He overcame blindness and political disappointment to write his epic masterpiece *Paradise Lost*, concerning the Judeo-Christian story of the Fall of Man, in 1667.

Puritan control was responsible for closing the theatres for nearly 20 years until the Restoration of Charles II in 1660. Restoration drama primarily reflected the licentiousness of the Court by the use of broad satire, farce, wit and bawdy comedy.

In prose, the language of the Bible exerted a strong influence, most notably in the work of **John Bunyan** (1628–88), whose *Pilgrim's Progress* was more widely read than any book in English except the Bible itself. The diaries of **John Evelyn** (1620–1706) and **Samuel Pepys** (1633–1703) detailed the minutiae of everyday life at the time.

## 18C

The early development of the novel is probably best exemplified in the work of Daniel Defoe (1660–1731). While his *Journal of the Plague Year* is a lively but primarily factual piece of journalism, *Robinson Crusoe*, though it utilises similar reporting techniques, is entirely fiction. Defoe's style was imitated and developed by **Samuel Richardson** (1689–1761), **Henry Fielding** (1707–54) and **Laurence Sterne** (1713–68).

The rise of the novel, the newspaper) and the expansion of a newly literate middle class were part of the Age of Reason. **Alexander Pope** (1688–1744), the finest satirical poet of the time, was matched in both poetry and prose by **Jonathan Swift** (1667–1745), famous for the incisive political and social satire of *Gulliver's Travels*. The era was dominated, however, by the influence of **Samuel Johnson** (1709–84), the subject of Boswell's famous biography and author of the first *English Dictionary* in 1755.

## 19C

The French Revolution was a primary inspiration for the Romantic movement, which stressed intensity of emotion and freedom of expression. This rebellious spirit was epitomised in the life of **Lord Byron** (1788–1824) though perhaps a better representative of Romantic poetry is **William Wordsworth** (1770–1850), whose best poems reflect his belief that intense joy could arise from deep harmony with Nature. **Percy Bysshe Shelley** (1792–1822) wrote more directly of the power of joy as a reforming influence, while the intense, lyrical verse of **John Keats** (1795–1821) stressed the power of beauty. Though

*Charles Dickens*

© UPPA/Photoshot

lyricism, nature and the exotic continued to attract Victorian poets such as **Robert Browning** (1812–89), faith in joy and the senses waned and the verse of **Alfred, Lord Tennyson** (1809–1902) is noble but sombre.

The novel, meanwhile, had continued to develop in range and appeal from the carefully structured domestic comedies of **Jane Austen** (1775–1817) to the more popular, if less deep, historical novels of her contemporary, **Sir Walter Scott** (1771–1832). Popular too were Scott's Victorian successors, **William Makepeace Thackeray** (1811–63), **Anthony Trollope** (1815–82) and, above all, **Charles Dickens** (1812–70), whose sentimental but funny and sometimes despairing vision of city life in the Industrial Revolution struck a sharp chord with the reading public. Mary Ann Evans (1819–80), under the pseudonym **George Eliot**, wrote realistic works about the problems of the provincial middle class. The **Brontë** sisters, **Charlotte** (1816–55) and **Emily** (1818–48), took inspiration from their upbringing on the wild moors of Yorkshire to write their respective masterpieces, *Jane Eyre* (1846) and *Wuthering Heights* (1847). Most important of the writers of the century is **Thomas Hardy** (1840–1928), whose novels express a passion for man's tragic involvement in Nature and estrangement from it.

Influenced by the new drama in Europe, **George Bernard Shaw** (1856–1950) brought a new purpose and seriousness to the English theatre which had, for nearly two centuries, failed to find a clear direction. The witty comedies of **Oscar Wilde** (1854–1900) were less profound but equally well crafted. They reflected the aims of the Decadent movement, which stressed flagrantly amoral beauty – a direct reaction against Victorian moral earnestness.

## 20C

The early modern masters of the **novel** – **Henry James** (1843–1916), **Joseph Conrad** (1857–1924) and **E M Forster** (1879–1970) – were still working in a recognisably Victorian tradition. The Dubliner **James Joyce** (1882–1941) used the stream-of-consciousness technique in the highly experimental *Ulysses* (1922) and *Finnegans Wake* (1939). This insistent excavation of personal experience is also found in the very different novels of **Virginia Woolf** (1882–1941) and of **D H Lawrence** (1885–1930), who challenged the taboos of class and sex, particularly in his novel *Lady Chatterley's Lover*. Concurrent with the serious "literary" novel, there developed a growing market for lighter fiction – entertainments – to serve the needs of an increasingly literate public; from the adventure novels of **Robert Louis Stevenson** (1850–94) and the *Sherlock Holmes* stories of **Arthur Conan Doyle** (1859–1930) to the spy thrillers of John Le Carré and Len Deighton in our own time. **George Orwell**'s (1903–50) dark political novels *(Animal Farm, 1984)* condemned the evils of communism.

Throughout the century there have been a number of important and stylish writers – less iconoclastic than their more innovative peers – who have continued to work with more traditional subjects and themes. The novelists **Aldous Huxley** (1894–1963), **Evelyn Waugh** (1903–66), and **Graham Greene** (1904–91) achieved considerable critical as well as commercial success, while **Somerset Maugham** (1874–1965) and **J B Priestley** (1894–1984) triumphed equally as playwrights and novelists. The novel has, in all its forms, become the dominant vehicle of literary expression in the modern age. Eminent contemporary writers include Anthony Powell (A Dance to the Music of Time); Paul Scott ((1920–78) The Raj Quartet and Staying On); **Anthony Burgess** (A Clockwork Orange and Earthly Powers), Lawrence Durrell (Alexandria Quartet (1957); William Golding, Lord of the Flies (1954) and Rites of Passage (1980), studies of human behaviour, Iris Murdoch ((1919–99) Under the Net and The Sea, The Sea, which deal with complex psychological issues), John Fowles' haunting stories (The French Lieutenant's Woman and The Magus). Doris Lessing (The Golden Notebook), Muriel Spark (The Prime of Miss Jean Brodie), **Daphne du Maurier** (Rebecca and Jamaica Inn) and Olivia Manning (The Balkan Trilogy) are also distinguished authors.

Among the new generation of writers who have won acclaim are **Martin Amis** (London Fields and The Information), Julian Barnes (The History of the World in 10½ Chapters), J G Ballard (The Empire of the Sun, Crash and Cocaine Nights), Angela Carter (Wise Children and The Magic Toyshop), A S Byatt (Possession), Anita Brookner (Hotel du Lac), Beryl Bainbridge (Every Man for Himself), Jeanette Winterson (Oranges Are Not the Only Fruit), Graham Swift (Last Orders), Pat Barker (Regeneration Trilogy), Irvine Welsh (Trainspotting).

**J K Rowling** almost single-handedly revived the children's adventure story (in the process becoming richer than the Queen) and introduced a new generation of children to reading with her record-breaking Harry Potter series.

The English-language tradition is enriched by writers from the Commonwealth and other countries who bring different perceptions: V S Naipaul, Caryl Phillips from the Caribbean, Nadine Gordimer, André Brink, J M Coetzee, Ben Okri from Africa; Peter Carey, Thomas Keneally, J G Ballard from Australia, Keri Hume from New Zealand, **Salman Rushdie**, Vikram Seth, Arundhati Roy from the Indian subcontinent and Kazuo Ishiguro from Japan.

**Poetry**, comparatively speaking, is less widely read than in previous times.

The Romantic decadence of the early-20C was swept aside by the Modernist poets **Ezra Pound** (1885–1972) and **T S Eliot** (1888–1965), whose The Waste Land (1922) is a dense and highly literary meditation on the situation of modern man. Less dramatically modern but equally influential was the slightly earlier poetry of **Thomas Hardy** and **W B Yeats** (1865–1939). The poets of the First World War, particularly **Wilfred Owen** (1893–1918) and **Siegfried Sassoon** (1886–1967), voiced their horror of mass warfare. **W H Auden** (1907–73) led a prominent group of intellectual left-wing poets in the 1920s and the exuberant imagery and lyrical rhetoric of **Dylan Thomas** (1914–53) caught the public's imagination. Only**John Betjeman** (1906–84), has achieved comparable popularity in recent times. Philip Larkin (1922–91) was the leading figure of the Movement group; the tone and form of his poetry expressing melancholic sensibilities in reaction to the romantic excesses of the 1940s. Poet Laureate Ted Hughes (1930–98), known for his violent and symbolic nature poems, is one of the most influential contemporary poets alongside Tom Paulin, Andrew Motion, Roger McGough, Benjamin Zephaniah, Carol Ann Duffy, Wendy Cope and Helen Dunmore.

The **theatre** of the first half of the century was dominated by well-crafted "traditional" plays and the sophisticated comedies of Noël Coward. In the 1950s The Theatre of the Absurd, which saw man as a helpless creature in a meaningless universe, was explored by the Irish writer **Samuel Beckett** (1906–89). Later in the decade, disillusionment with contemporary Britain was vented by **John Osborne** (1929–94) in his play Look Back in Anger. The pithy "comedies of menace" by **Harold Pinter** (1930–2008) and the socialist plays of writers such as **Arnold Wesker** (b.1932) subsequently led to the development of a diverse and challenging contemporary theatre. Trenchant plays by Edward Bond, Peter Shaffer, Alan Ayckbourn, David Hare and Tom Stoppard are still stalwarts in the British theatre season with strong attendance.

# Nature

**The exceptionally diverse geological foundation of Britain has given rise to landscapes of great variety, a natural heritage enhanced by a continuous human presence over several millennia which has shaped and reshaped the material to form the present uniquely rich pattern of fields and fells, woods and parks, villages and farmsteads. Celebrated in literature and art, this densely textured landscape, usually domesticated but with its wilder beauties too, has become a kind of national emblem, lived in lovingly and vigorously defended against change by its inhabitants.**

## LANDSCAPE

The country can be broadly divided into **Upland** and **Lowland** Britain. The former, generally of older, harder material, comprises much of the North and Southwest of England and virtually the whole of Wales and Scotland. As well as rolling, open moorlands, where the eye ranges freely over vast expanses of coarse grass, bracken or heather, there are mountain chains, modest in elevation but exhibiting most of the features of much higher and more extensive systems, attracting serious climbers as well as walkers.

To the south and east the gentler relief of Lowland Britain is mostly composed of less resistant material. Much is "scarp and vale" country where undulating chalk and limestone hills terminate in steep escarpments commanding grand panoramas over broad clay vales.

Most of the course of the Earth's history can be traced in these landscapes. From the unimaginably distant Pre-Cambrian, more than 600 million years ago, came the Torridonian sandstone and Lewisian gneiss of northwest Scotland as well as the compact, isolated uplands of Charnwood Forest in Leicestershire and the Malvern Hills in Worcestershire. The violent volcanic activity of Ordovician times left the shales and slates of **Snowdonia** and the **Lake District**. Extreme pressure

from the Southeast in the Caledonian mountain-building period produced the northeast/southwest "grain" of ridges and valleys so evident in much of Wales and Scotland. Most of the abundant reserves of coal originated in the tropical vegetation of Carboniferous times. Except for the extreme south, the whole country was affected by the action of the often immensely thick ice sheets of the series of Ice Ages. The characteristically sculpted forms of the high mountains testify to the great power of the glaciers as they advanced and retreated, eroding and transporting vast quantities of material, much of which was spread over the lowlands by the mighty ancestors of today's rivers. As the last of the ice melted, the sea level rose, the land bridge joining Britain to the continent of Europe was flooded, and a truncated **Thames**, hitherto a tributary of the Rhine, acquired its own outlet to the sea.

## DOMESTICATION

The taming and settling of the landscape can be traced back to the 5th millennium BC when Neolithic farmers began to clear the wildwood, the dense forests which had spread northwards in the wake of the retreating ice. The imprint of each succeeding age may be traced, not only in the obvious features of prehistoric stone circles, burial mounds and hill-forts, the planned network of Roman roads or the countless medieval churches, but also in the everyday fabric of the working countryside, where a track may first have been trodden in the Bronze Age or a hedge planted by Saxon settlers.

The many-layered landscape is now characterised by **enclosure**, a web of fields bounded by hedges in the lowlands, by drystone walls in the uplands and by dykes in areas reclaimed from the sea. Small fields with irregular boundaries are likely to be ancient in origin; a regular chequerboard of hawthorn hedges is the result of agricultural "improvement" in the 18C and 19C.

In spite of conditions which are ideal for tree growth, only eight percent of

## National Parks

🍂 *See the Discovering section.*
Britain's 15 national parks
comprise the Brecon
Beacons, the Broads (Norfolk
and Suffolk), Cairngorms,
Dartmoor, Exmoor, Lake
District, Loch Lomond, New
Forest, North York Moors,
Northumberland, Peak
District, Pembrokeshire
Coast, Snowdonia, South
Downs, Yorkshire Dales.
These comprise the finest
upland scenery in the
country, much of it farmed
and in private ownership,
controlled and managed by
each national park authority
to conserve the characteristic
landscape and make it
accessible to the public.
The first national park
was established in 1951 to
preserve the distinctive
characteristics of certain
rural areas of England and
Wales. The scheme was not
extended to Scotland,
where the law of trespass
was different, enabling
people to walk where they
wished provided they did
no damage.
*For more information visit
www.nationalparks.gov.uk.*

the land surface is wooded. About half
of this consists of recent coniferous
plantations, mostly in the uplands. In
many parts of the lowlands, the lack
of great forests is compensated for by
an abundance of small woods and by
the countless individual trees growing
in parks and gardens, and above all, in
the hedgerows.

Standing out from this orderly pattern
are the "commons", rough open tracts
of grass and scrub. Once the villager's
source of fodder, food and game, they
now provide fresh air and exercise for
both town and country people.

The country is well watered. The abundant rainfall, carried off the hills by a
multitude of streams, feeds the rivers
which, though of no great length, often
end in splendid estuaries which bring
salt water and the feel of the sea far
inland.

The irregular outline of the country and
the complex geology combine to form
a long and varied coastline. Where the
mountains meet the sea there is exceptionally fine coastal scenery, such as the
spectacular chalk-white cliffs near Dover,
symbol of English insularity. Many of the
better stretches of sand and shingle have
been appropriated by seaside resorts
but there are some quieter beaches as
well as remote marshlands and lonely
sand dunes.

View of Llynnau Mymbyr and Mount Snowdon, Snowdonia, Wales
© Jon Arnold/hemis.fr

London is not only the commercial, political and artistic capital of the United Kingdom, but also one of the great financial centres and tourist destinations of the world. The City of London ("The City") deals in trade and commerce while the City of Westminster, incorporating the West End, is famous for its royal palaces and parliament, theatres, entertainment, art and fashion.

## A Bit of History

London first began to take shape under the Romans, who made it the hub of their road system. They enclosed it with walls and built the first London Bridge. Remains of the Roman walls, together with medieval additions, are still visible on the street called London Wall and near the Tower of London.

It was Edward the Confessor (1042–66) who established the rival centre at Westminster, when he built a royal palace and founded an abbey, its minster in the west, as opposed to St Paul's Cathedral, its minster in the east.

In fact London did not become the official capital of England until the mid-12C, taking over from Winchester. The City and its busy port gained considerable freedom and independence from the crown, which was often dependent on City merchants for raising money for military expeditions. The great houses of the nobility lined the Strand along the north bank of the Thames, while merchants built elegant mansions in the less crowded West End, or nearby villages like Islington, Holborn and Chelsea.

Overcrowding was somewhat reduced by the ravages of the Great Plague (1665), in which 75,000 out of 460,000 people died, and of the Great Fire (1666), which destroyed 80 percent of the buildings. Within six days of the end of the fire, Christopher Wren, then 33 years old, submitted a plan to rebuild the city with broad straight streets. It was rejected, though Wren was commissioned to build the new St Paul's Cathedral and the majority of the city's churches.

As the population continued to expand, poor-quality housing proliferated, accompanied by limited investment in sanitation. The appalling conditions of the 18C are strikingly illustrated in the work of William Hogarth. Charles Dickens continued to document the poverty and dreadful living conditions well into the 19C. Eventually in 1855 the government established the Metropolitan Board of Works, a central body with special responsibility for mains sewerage, and the tide of filth began to turn.

Destruction was to again play a role in the modernisation of the city when the piles of rubble left by German bombers during The Blitz of 1940–41 provided opportunities for modern and imaginative redevelopment such as the arts centres at the South Bank Arts Centre and the Barbican.

▶ **Population:** 7,556,900.

◔ **Michelin Map:**
Michelin Atlas pp19–21
or map 504 T 29.

▤ **Info:** For tourist information, ◔ see the Addresses.

◑ **Location:** Most sightseeing and tourist activities are confined to Westminster, the West End and Kensington. The Underground is the most effective way of getting around town, though buses will allow you to see more. Taxis are expensive. Always catch a licensed taxi cab. Short distances are best covered on foot. There are various bus sightseeing tours, of which The Big Bus Company (☎020 7233 9533; www.bigbustours. com) is among the best. Public buses run throughout the UK from Victoria Coach Station, a short walk from Victoria underground station and Buckingham Palace. Trains run from:

## London Today

The City remains a financial power-house, thronged with pin-striped suits by day but deserted by night and on weekends. Its itinerant citizens almost all commute to the suburbs or much farther afield. The rest of London, and particularly the West End, is lively at all hours – by day with shoppers and office workers and by night with people going to the theatres, pubs, restaurants and nightclubs. London has grown organically over the centuries absorbing other towns and villages as it sprawls ever outwards. Most Londoners live in the old belt of "villages" (such as Hampstead, Chiswick, Kensington or Chelsea), which have retained their own character.

The cosmopolitan atmosphere of London was greatly reinforced in the latter half of the 20C by easier foreign travel, higher standards of living, immigration from the former Empire and Britain's membership of the European Union; as reflected in the large number of foreign restaurants and food stores. Modern multicultural London has many of its own traditions from Hindu Diwali to the **Notting Hill Carnival** (last weekend of Aug), London's biggest festival and the second-largest street festival after Rio. Between one and two million visitors turn this area of London into a giant free party each year.

The 1980s and 90s saw the large-scale regeneration of 8sq mi/21sq km of derelict warehouses and dock basins east of The City in the **Docklands**, which were converted into offices of epic proportions; at 774ft/236m, Canary Wharf Tower is the tallest building in the UK. Around the Docklands modern flats, low-rise housing and sports facilities have been laid out. More recently, the Swiss Re Building and London Bridge's Shard have joined the skyline.

A massive building programme has seen the creation of the **2012 Olympic Park**. The Olympic Park in the Lea Valley, just east of the Docklands, is one of the largest construction and engineering projects in Europe. It features the Aquatics Centre, Hockey Stadium, Multi-sport arenas, 80,000-seat Olympic Stadium and Velopark, as well as the Olympic Village and Media Centre.

Euston and King's Cross/ St Pancras (northern destinations and Eurostar); Paddington and Marylebone (western destinations); Waterloo, Victoria and London Bridge (the south); and Liverpool Street and Fenchurch Street (the east).

- **Don't Miss:** The London Eye; British Museum; National Gallery; Covent Garden; Westminster Abbey; St Paul's Cathedral; Natural History Museum; Science Museum; Tower of London; Kew Gardens; Hampton Court Palace; Greenwich (by river boat); London Zoo.
- **Kids:** Most major London attractions are good for families and kids; look for the Kids symbol in the following pages.
- **Walking Tours:** There are many walking tour operators; the best is the Original London Walks (*020 7624 3978; www.walks.com*).

## Traditional London

Tradition still plays an important role in London life. The ceremonial **Changing of the Guard** at Buckingham Palace (*summer daily 11.30am, in summer; otherwise every other day*) and **Horse Guards** (*Mon–Sat 11am, Sun 10am*) draw the crowds. There is more pageantry and military precision when the Queen attends **Trooping the Colour** on Horse Guards Parade (*2nd or 3rd Sat in Jun*) and the **State Opening of Parliament** (*Nov*). In the **Lord Mayor's Show** (*2nd Sat in Nov*) the newly elected Lord Mayor of London proceeds through The City in the Golden State Coach before taking his oath at the Royal Courts of Justice in the Strand.

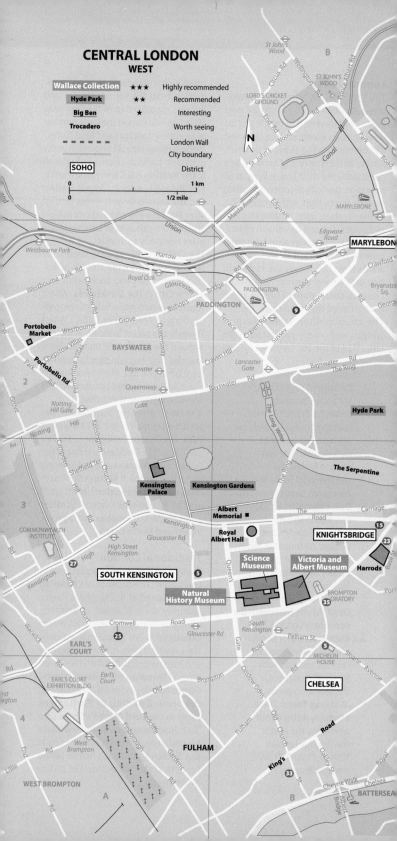

# CENTRAL LONDON
## WEST

| | | |
|---|---|---|
| **Wallace Collection** | ★★★ | Highly recommended |
| **Hyde Park** | ★★ | Recommended |
| **Big Ben** | ★ | Interesting |
| **Trocadero** | | Worth seeing |
| – – – – – | | London Wall |
| | | City boundary |
| **SOHO** | | District |

0 — 1 km
0 — 1/2 mile

**N**

B

St John's Wood

LORD'S CRICKET GROUND

St John's Wood

MARYLEBONE

Edgware Road

**MARYLEBON**

Westbourne Park

Union

Harrow

Road

Crawford

Bryanston Sq.

Georg

Westbourne Park Rd

Royal Oak

Gloucester

Bishop's

Bridge

PADDINGTON

Praed St.

Gardens

9

Chepstow Villas

Westbourne

Grove

Queensway

Terrace

Craven Rd

Sussex

**Portobello Market**

**BAYSWATER**

Bayswater

Craven Hill

Lancaster Gate

Bayswater Rd

The Ring

**Portobello Rd**

Pembridge Villas

Queensway

Bayswater Rd

Park Rd

Notting Hill Gate

Gate

The Long Water

**Hyde Park**

Grove

Notting Hill

Av.

Campden Hill

Church

Kensington

**The Serpentine**

Sheffield Ter.

The Ring

**Kensington Palace**

**Kensington Gardens**

The Road

Carriage

COMMONWEALTH INSTITUTE

High Street Kensington

St

Kensington

**Albert Memorial** ■

**KNIGHTSBRIDGE**

15

23

27

Gloucester Rd

**Royal Albert Hall** ●

**SOUTH KENSINGTON**

5

**Science Museum**

**Victoria and Albert Museum**

**Harrods**

**Natural History Museum**

Queen's

BROMPTON ORATORY

35

Por

High

Earl's

Kensington

Cromwell

Road

Gloucester Rd

South Kensington

Pelham St.

25

Gate Rd

**CHELSEA**

5

MICHELIN HOUSE

Warwick

EARL'S COURT

Earl's Court

Old

Brompton

Sloane Avenue

Rd

EARL'S COURT EXHIBITION BLDG

Earl's Court

Redcliffe

Fulham

Onslow Gdns

Old Church

Road

**King's**

Road

Oakley St.

West Brompton

Finborough

Gardens

**FULHAM**

King's

33

St

Cheyne Walk

Chelsea

**WEST BROMPTON**

A

B

Albert Bridge

**BATTERSEA**

2

3

4

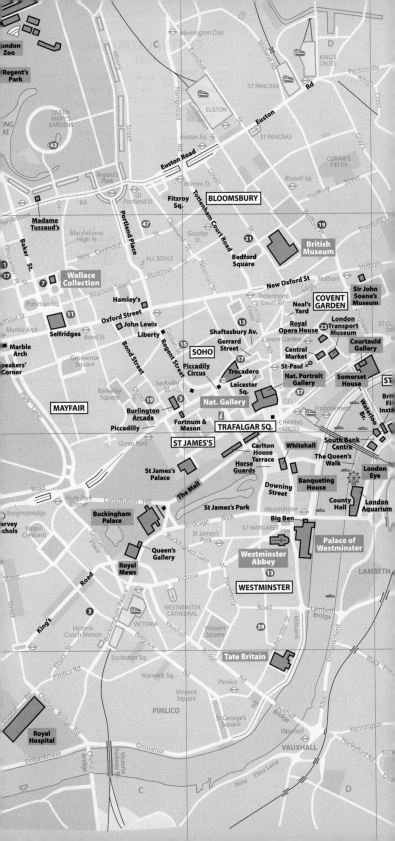

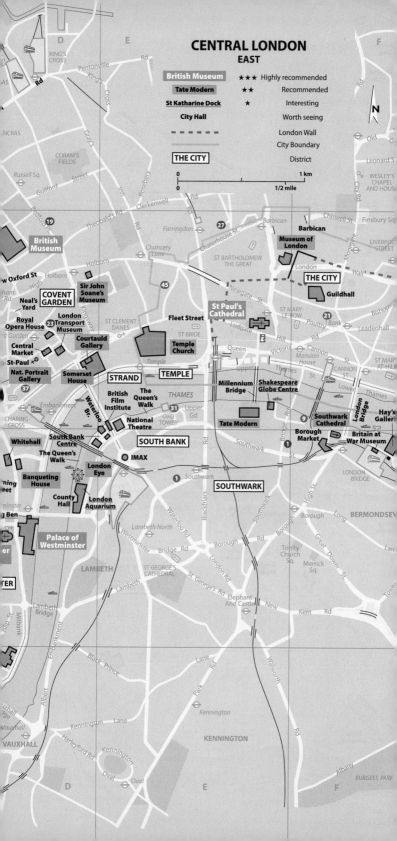

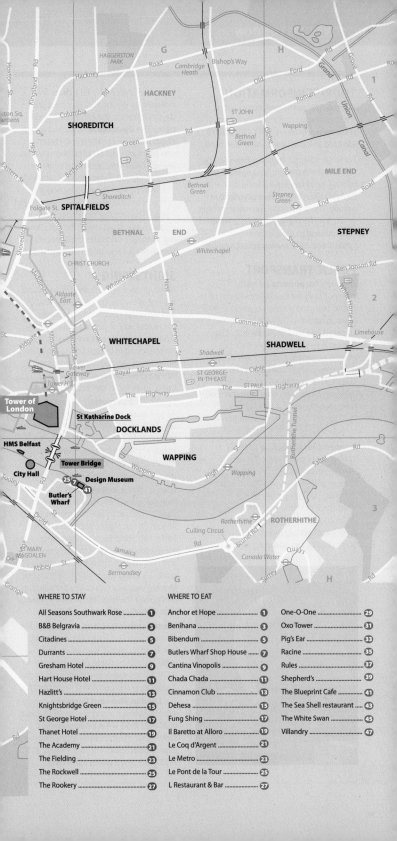

## WHERE TO STAY

## WHERE TO EAT

## TOURIST INFORMATION

The main tourist information point is the Britain and London Visitor Centre *(1 Lower Regent Street, SW1Y 4NS; ℘0870 156 6366 (infoline); www.visitlondon.com)*.

For what is happening specifically in The City (London's ancient Square Mile), go to the City of London Information Centre *(St Paul's Churchyard; www.cityoflondon. gov.uk)*. There are also information centres at Twickenham *(℘020 8891 7272; www. visitrichmond.co.uk)* and Greenwich *(℘0870 608 2000; www.greenwich.gov.uk)*.

## PUBLIC TRANSPORT

London's five **airports** are each connected to the city by some form of public transport. Express trains to central London run from Gatwick, Heathrow, Stansted and Luton (shuttle first). City Airport is by far the most central but is business oriented and only services a limited number of European cities. The most enjoyable way of travelling to France or Brussels is by **Eurostar** *(www.eurostar.com)*, a high-speed train service from St Pancras station to the continent via the Eurotunnel.

**Transport for London** *(℘0843 222 1234; www.tfl.gov.uk)* runs the tube (Underground), buses, Docklands Light Railway and Thames riverboats, while regional train companies service the majority of the suburbs, particularly in south London. The **journey planner** on *(www.tfl.gov.uk)* should be your first point of call when planning day trips.

Oyster card
©Transport for London

Individual and combined **tickets** are available by the journey, day, multiple days or longer, suitable for every kind of travel. The **Oyster card** *(http://visitorshop. tfl.gov.uk)* is the cheapest and easiest way to travel, valid on all public transport (except taxis). This credit card ticket can be used repeatedly and loaded with virtually any fare. They can be bought online or are available at any Underground station. The simplest option for most visitors is to top-up credit; the card then automatically calculates the cheapest overall ticket for journeys made that day.

## SIGHTSEEING

Although by its nature, the Underground will not allow you to see the true layout and character of London, it is usually the fastest way of getting around town. If possible, you should avoid using the Underground in central London at rush hours. If you are touring Westminster you are often better off walking or using buses for longer hops.

Certain TFL **bus routes**, such as the no. 11, give a fantastic tour of the city for very little money. Be warned, though, in Westminster, buses may require you to buy a ticket before you board. Bus drivers generally do accept cash, but usually only coins; use an Oyster instead.

Tours on **open-topped buses** start from Victoria, Green Park, Piccadilly, Coventry Street, Trafalgar Square, Haymarket, Lower Regent Street, Marble Arch, Baker Street, Tower Hill. Some tours are non-stop; some allow passengers to hop on or off and continue on a later bus. For details of guided walking tours, visit the Britain and London Visitor Centre or see press listings, particularly the excellent weekly magazine *Time Out (www.timeout.com/london)*.

**Thames cruises** start from Westminster Pier, Charing Cross Pier, Tower Pier, Greenwich Pier. Evening cruises with music and/or a meal are also available. River transport is still the most expensive branch of London Transport, but is becoming more popular.

The **London Waterbus Company** operates a regular service along the Regent's Canal *(t020 7482 2550; www.londonwaterbus. com)*. Other operators are Jason's Trip *(www.jasons.co.uk)* and Jenny Wren *℘020 7485 4433; (www.walkersquay.com)*.

# Westminster★★★

## SIGHTS

### Westminster Abbey★★★

⊖*Westminster. Abbey:* ⏱*General opening times: year-round Mon–Fri 9.30am–4.30pm, Wed until 7pm (winter 6pm), Sat until 2pm; last entry 1hr before closing. Sun for services only. In winter hours may be reduced, see website for details.* ⌕*£16 (inc entry to all areas below).* ⌖ *Guided tours £3.* ♿. ☎*020 7222 7110. Cloister:* ⏱*Open daily 8am–6pm. Chapter House, Pyx Chamber and Abbey Museum:* ⏱*Open daily 10.30am–3.30pm/4pm.* ⏱*Closed 1 Jan, 24–26 Dec and except services. College Garden:* ⏱*Open Tue–Thu, 10am–6pm (4pm Oct–Mar). Brass band concerts in garden (⌕free) Jul–Aug 12.30pm–2pm (☎020 7654 4900). www.westminster-abbey.org.*

The abbey, in which William the Conqueror was crowned as **William I** on Christmas Day 1066, and in which **Prince William married Kate Middleton** on 29 April 2011, was built by **Edward the Confessor** in the Norman style. It was only after the rebuilding by the Plantagenet Henry III in 1220 that it acquired its present Gothic appearance. Henry III began with the Lady Chapel, to provide a noble shrine for the Confessor, who had been canonised in 1163. Gradually the existing building was demolished as new replaced the old. When Henry VII constructed his **chapel** at the east end (1503–19) he produced the jewel of the age. The west towers by Wren and Nicholas Hawksmoor (1722–45) and repairs by George Gilbert Scott kept to the Gothic spirit.

Inside, the vaulting is glorious, the carving on screens and arches delicate, often beautiful, sometimes humorous; the ancient tombs in **Henry VII's**, **St Edward's** and the ambulatory chapels are dignified. The transepts and aisles adorned with sculpted monuments, particularly in the famous **Poets' Corner★** *(south transept)*, where there are monuments to many great poets though few are actually buried here; the tomb of Geoffrey Chaucer was the first in this corner, others interred here include Alfred Lord Tennyson and Robert Browning.

The **sanctuary** beyond the **choir** is where the **coronation ceremony** is performed. To the right hangs a 16C tapestry behind a large 15C altarpiece of rare beauty. Beyond is an ancient 13C sedilia painted with full-length royal figures (Henry III, Edward I). The **Henry VII Chapel★★★** with its superb fan-vaulted roof is the most glorious of the abbey's many treasures. The banners of the Knights Grand Cross of the **Order of the Bath** hang still and brilliant above the stalls with inventive 16C–18C misericords. The **Chapel of Edward the Confessor★★** is rich in history, with the Confessor's shrine ringed with the tombs of five kings and three queens. In the centre against a carved stone **screen** (1441) stands the Coronation Chair, which until recently contained the Stone of Scone beneath the seat (⌖*see EDINBURGH and PERTH*). The **Chapter House★★** (1248–53) is an octagonal vaulted chamber (60ft/18m in diameter) with Purbeck marble columns. Its walls are partially decorated with medieval paintings.

Westminster Abbey

©Galen Goyer/iStockphoto.com

## Palace of Westminster (Houses of Parliament)★★★

⊖*Westminster.* ↻*Open Aug–Sept (summer recess) by guided tour (75min) starting from the Victoria Tower. UK residents can tour throughout the year; overseas visitors may only tour on Sat and during the Summer Opening.* ◉*£15. Book tickets on* ✆*0844 847 1672 or via www.ticketmaster.co.uk. Advance booking strongly advised, available from March onwards. When Parliament is in session the general public are allowed into the Visitors' Gallery free of charge to watch the proceedings in the House of Commons. Be prepared to queue for popular sessions, such as Prime Minister's Question Time, If you do not have advance tickets. www.parliament.uk.*

The palace built by Edward the Confessor was enlarged and embellished by the medieval English kings but most of the surviving buildings, by then occupied by Parliament, were destroyed in a disastrous fire in 1834. The oldest part is **Westminster Hall**★★, which William Rufus added to his father's palace between 1097 and 1099. This scene of royal banquets and jousts in the Middle Ages was altered and re-roofed by command of Richard II between 1394 and 1399. For this the upper parts were rebuilt and what is perhaps the finest timber roof of all time was built, a superb **hammerbeam**★★★ designed by the king's master carpenter, Hugh Herland. After the 1834 fire, which, fortunately, did not damage Westminster Hall, **Charles Barry** and **Augustus Pugin** won a competition for a new design for the palace, which became known as the Houses of Parliament. Together they created a masterpiece of Victorian Gothic architecture. It was completed in 1860, with over 1,000 rooms, 100 staircases and 2mi/3km of corridors over 8 acres/3ha.

The Clock Tower (316ft/96m), the most famous feature of this distinctive building, was completed by 1859. The name **Big Ben**★ applied originally to the great bell, probably so-called after Sir Benjamin Hall, the Commissioner of

Works and a man of considerable girth. The clock, which has an electrically wound mechanism, proved reliable for 117 years, until it succumbed to metal fatigue in 1976 when it required major repairs. Big Ben was first broadcast on New Year's Eve 1923 and its chimes are the most famous in the world.

The **House of Commons**★, rebuilt after being bombed in 1941, seats 437 of the 659 elected Members of Parliament; at the end of this simply decorated chamber is the canopied Speaker's Chair. Red stripes on both sides of the green carpet mark the limit to which a Member may advance to address the House – the distance between the stripes is reputedly that of two drawn swords.

The **House of Lords**★★ is a masterpiece of design and workmanship. The throne and steps, beneath a Gothic canopy mounted on a wide screen, all in gold, occupies one end of the chamber. The ceiling is divided by ribs and gold patterning above the leather benches and the Woolsack, seat of the Lord Chancellor since the reign of Edward III, adopted as a symbol of the importance to England of the wool trade.

## Whitehall★★

The wide street, which leads north from Parliament Square and Parliament Street, is lined by government offices. In the middle stands the Cenotaph, the austere war memorial designed by Sir Edwin Lutyens. On the left is **Downing Street** (*no public access*) where a relatively modest Georgian house (no. 10) has been the official residence of the prime minister since 1732. **Banqueting House**★★ (⊖*Westminster;* ↻*open (government functions permitting) Mon–Sat 10am–5pm;* ↻*closed Good Fri, 1 Jan, 24–26 Dec, and bank hols;* ◉*£5;* ♿*;* ✆*0844 482 7777; www.hrp.org. uk*), the only part of the great Whitehall Palace to survive destruction by fire, was designed by Inigo Jones in 1619, but much altered in the early-19C. The hall is a double cube with a delicate balcony on gilded corbels; the ceiling is divided by richly decorated beams into compartments filled with magnificent

*Houses of Parliament*

©David Joyner/iStockphoto.com

paintings (1634–35) by Rubens. It was on a platform erected in front of this building that Charles I was executed in January 1649.

Opposite stands **Horse Guards**★ famous for the presence of the **Household Cavalry sentries**. The ceremonial mounting of the **Queen's Life Guard**★★★ occurs daily at 11am (10am Sun) in summer on Horse Guards Parade. The dismount ceremony is daily at 4pm in the Front Yard of Horse Guards. The cavalry rides along The Mall between Horse Guards and their barracks in Hyde Park. Behind is the parade ground, where Trooping the Colour takes place in June.

## St James's Park★★

⊖St James's Park.

The oldest and most beautiful royal park in London dates from 1532 when Henry VIII had **St James's Palace** built. The park was landscaped in the 19C by John Nash, who was also responsible for the majestic **Carlton House Terrace**★ in the northeast corner. From the bridge over the water there is a fine **view** of Whitehall and Buckingham Palace.

## Buckingham Palace★★

⊖St James's Park, Victoria.
🕙Open late Jul–late Sept/early Oct daily 9.30am–6.30pm (4.15pm last entry) by timed ticket only. ☞£18. Joint ticket with Royal Mews and Queen's

Gallery £31.95. ♿. ✆020 776 7300. www.royalcollection.org.uk.

Buckingham House was built by the Duke of Buckingham in 1703 and purchased in 1762 by George III. Under George IV it was converted into a palace (1825–37) by John Nash and Edward Blore; the east front containing the famous balcony was added in 1847. The tour includes Throne Room, Drawing Rooms, Dining Room and the Picture Gallery, hung with royal portraits and old masters (*Charles I* Van Dyck; portraits by Rembrandt and Frans Hals; seascapes by Van de Velde; *A Lady at the Virginals*, Vermeer; pastoral and religious scenes by Rubens…) and furnished with many pieces collected by George IV.

When the sovereign is in residence, the Royal Standard flies over the palace.

The **Changing of the Guard**★★ (🕙*takes place usually May–end Jul/early–Aug daily 11.30am; except in very poor weather, rest of year alternate days at 11.30am. www.changing-the-guard. com*) takes place in the palace forecourt. Arrive early for a good view.

The **Queen's Gallery**★★ (*separate entrance;* 🕙*open daily 9.30am/10am–5.30pm by timed ticket (last entry 4.30pm),* ☞£9.25; ♿; ✆020 7766 7301; www.royalcollection.org.uk) exhibits portraits, paintings, drawings and furniture in the priceless Royal Collection.

# West End★★

## TRAFALGAR SQUARE★★

⊖Charing Cross.

Begun in 1829, the square was completed in the 1840s, when Charles Barry levelled it and built the north terrace for the National Gallery (●see below). In 1842 **Nelson's Column** was erected; the monument is 185ft/56m tall, with the pedestal, fluted granite column, bronze capital and a 17ft/5.2m statue of the great admiral who lost his life in victory at the Battle of Trafalgar.

Note the equestrian statue *(south)* of **Charles I** cast by Le Sueur in 1633. A plaque in the road next to it marks the spot from where all road distances to/from London are measured. Ironically the square is now pedestrianised. Note the four plinths at each corner of the square. While three of these are occupied by conventional historical statues, the fourth plinth is now the location for specially commissioned artworks.

The church of **St Martin-in-the-Fields**★ *(Trafalgar Square;* ○*open daily 8am–6pm;* ⚐*guided tour twice monthly Thu 11.30am;* &✗; ✆*020 7766 1100; www. stmartin-in-the-fields.org)* was built by James Gibbs in 1722–26, with a Corinthian portico and elegant spire. Today it is one of London's most active churches, staging free **lunchtime recitals** *(Mon–Tue and Fri at 1pm;* ⊜£3.50 donation suggested)*; **classical concerts** *(Thu–Sat 7.30pm;* is home to the **London Brass Rubbing Centre** *(Mon–Sat 10am–6pm/8pm, Sun 11.30am–5pm;* and the award-winning Café in the Crypt restaurant.

## National Gallery★★★

⊖*Leicester Square, Charing Cross. Trafalgar Square.* ○*Open year-round daily 10am–6pm (9pm Fri).* ○*Closed 1 Jan, 24–26 Dec.* ⊜*Charge only for temporary exhibitions.* ⚐*Guided tour (1hr) daily at 11.30am, 2.30pm, also 7pm Fri.* &✗. ✆*020 7747 2885. www.nationalgallery.org.uk.*

This landmark building was completed in 1838, its pedimented portico of Corinthian columns forming a climax to Trafal

gar Square. The sixth and latest extension to the original building is the Sainsbury Wing (1991) by Robert Venturi.

There are now more than 2,000 paintings in the collection; they represent the jewels in the public domain from early to High Renaissance Italian painting, early Netherlandish, German, Flemish, Dutch, French and Spanish pictures and masterpieces of the English 18C. The fuller representation of British art, particularly the more modern and 20C work of all schools. is in Tate Britain.

The galleries are arranged chronologically starting with the period 1260–1510 in the **Sainsbury Wing**. Leonardo's fragile preparatory "cartoon" of *Virgin and Child with St Anne and John the Baptist* is spectacular while his *Virgin of the Rocks* is similarly enigmatic and engaging. Uccello exploits strong lines and colour in his epic *Battle of San Romano.* Haunting realism and solemn stillness are the keywords in the works of Van Eyck and Van der Weyden, particularly in the former's legendary *Arnolfini Portrait.* Botticelli is represented by *Venus and Mars* and *Portrait of a Young Man* while other Italian masters in this gallery are Raphael, Mantegna and Bellini, whose perfect use of oils is encapsulated in his *Madonna and Child.* Earlier German and Netherlandish work is also represented by Dürer, Cranach, Bosch and Memlinc. Paintings in the **West Wing** range from 1510 to 1600. *The Ambassadors* by Holbein is a wonderful large-scale historical portrait and its famous *trompe l'œil* skull is a great favourite with gallery visitors. Tintoretto, El Greco, Michelangelo and Veronese are also here.

In the North Wing are paintings by the French school, the Spanish school and from the Low Countries. Works by Claude and the great British landscape artist J M W Turner are shown together and should not be missed. Rembrandt and Rubens, Caravaggio, Velázquez and Van Dyck (his huge *Equestrian Picture of Charles I* is unmissable) also star here. Paintings from 1700 to 1900 are exhibited in the **East Wing**. The British school is exemplified by classics such as *The Haywain* by Constable, *The Fighting*

*Temeraire* and *Rain, Steam and Speed* by J M W Turner. There are works by Canaletto, Goya, Tiepolo and Delacroix but many visitor's favourites are the Impressionist collection starring Pissarro, Renoir, Monet, Manet, Degas and Cézanne. Van Gogh's *Chair* and *Sunflowers* (once the world's most expensive painting) stand out as crowd pleasers. Seurat's *Bathers at Asnière* is another favourite. Another distinctive and popular artist is Henri Rousseau, whose *Tiger in a Tropical Storm* is a classic.

## National Portrait Gallery★★

⊖ *Leicester Square, Charing Cross. St Martin's Lane.* ⊙ *Open year-round daily 10am–6pm (9pm Thu–Fri).* ⊙ *Closed 24–26 Dec.* ✆ *Charge for temporary exhibitions only.* ♿✗. ✆ *020 7306 0055. www.npg.org.uk.*
Here you will find portraits of almost every British person of significant public or historical interest from the Middle Ages to the present day, some painted, sculpted or photographed by the famous artists of the day. They range from the raffish picture of **William Shakespeare** (his only known contemporary portrait) to Sir Winston Churchill and Margaret Thatcher to modern icons such as Diana, Princess of Wales and David Beckham.

## MAYFAIR★

The most luxurious district of London takes its name from a cattle and general fair held annually in May until it was closed in 1706 for unruly behaviour. It contains the most elegant hotels and the smartest shops in all of London: **Burlington Arcade**★ (1819), where the bow-fronted boutiques sell fashion, jewellery, leather goods; **Bond Street**★ famous for art auctioneers and dealers (Sotheby's, Phillips, Agnew's, Colnaghi), jewellery (Asprey, Cartier) and fashion (Fenwick, Yves St Laurent); **Regent Street** well known for elegant stores (Austin Reed, Aquascutum, Burberry, Jaeger and **Liberty**★★); **Oxford Street** lined with the more popular department stores (John Lewis, Debenhams, D H Evans, Selfridges and Marks & Spencer).

### River Cruises

There's no better way to spend a sunny day in London than an excursion to **Greenwich**★★★ by river cruiser from Westminster, Charing Cross or Tower Pier. Make sure you pick one with a live (rather than a pre-recorded) commentary. You can return a different route, by the foot tunnel under the Thames to Island Gardens. There is a fine **view**★★ of Greenwich Palace from Island Gardens on the north bank, which can be reached via the foot tunnel. From here return west on the Docklands Light Railway (DLR), enjoying the scenic ride on its elevated track (✆ *0843 7222 1234; www.tfl.gov.uk*).

Less well known is **Shepherd Market**, a charming maze of lanes, alleyways and paved courts linked by archways with a village atmosphere. Victorian and Edwardian pubs and houses, antique shops and small inserted shop fronts which serve in summer as pavement cafés line its streets.

You will find it hard to hear a nightingale singing in **Berkeley Square** (created 1737) these days but it is still a very impressive plane-tree-lined ensemble – the trees are not much younger, many dating from the late-1780s. Look for the late-18C houses on the west side with ironwork balconies, lamp holders at the steps and torch snuffers.

## Piccadilly Circus★

This famous road junction (circus), once considered the hub of the British Empire, is still dominated by **Eros**, the Angel of Christian Charity, surmounting the fountain erected in memory of the philanthropist Lord Shaftesbury in 1892. It is famous for its garish neon advertising hoardings and as a meeting place. Appropriately, London's gaudiest attraction, a branch of 👥**Ripley's Believe It or Not! Museum**★ (⊖ *Piccadilly Circus;* ⊙ *open year-round daily 10am–midnight, last entry 10.30pm;* ✆*£24.90, child £19.90 (both (inc.Mir-*

ror Maze) &✕; ℰ020 3238 0022; www.ripleyattractions.com) is located here and wows the crowds with its inimitable mixture of amazing facts and jaw-dropping artefacts.

Off the Circus, **Shaftesbury Avenue** is the heart of London "theatreland".

## MARYLEBONE
### Wallace Collection★★★
⊖Bond Street. Manchester Square. ⏱Open daily 10am–5pm. ⏱Closed 24–26 Dec. &✕. ℰ020 7563 9500. www.wallacecollection.org.

This gathering of one of the world's finer collections of 18C French art was the life's work of the 4th Marquess of Hertford (1800–70). These sit along Italian masters, 17C Dutch painting, 18C French furniture (note the magnificent cabinets by A C Boulle), and Sèvres porcelain. Don't miss the formidable display of European weapons and arms, nor **Gallery 22** hung with the larger 17C pictures and Old Master paintings including works by Rubens, Murillo, Velázquez, Rembrandt, Van Dyck, Gainsborough and the most popular work in the museum, *The Laughing Cavalier* by Frans Hals.

## ♟♟ COVENT GARDEN★★
Covent Garden Piazza, the first London square, was designed by Inigo Jones in 1631. It was originally surrounded by colonnades, long demolished.

**St Paul's Church** is an original survivor, its elegant portico dominating the west side of the square.

At the centre are the **Central Market Buildings★★**, designed in 1832 by Charles Fowler, to house the fruit and vegetable market, which moved out in 1974. The tiny shops and market stalls which now occupy it sell all kinds of goods, much of it aimed at visiting tourists (fashion, jewellery, crafts, etc.) and there are dozens of refreshment options. One of the biggest draws is the high-quality (licensed) musicians and street artists who perform on the open cobblestones.

Covent Garden has long been synonymous with opera, and its **Royal Opera**

**House**★ has been magnificently refurbished. Its design incorporates the original framework of the old Floral Hall.

Also recently revamped with great success, ♟♟**London Transport Museum**★ (⏱open Sat–Thu 10am–6pm, Fri 11am–6pm; ✍£13.50, child free; &✕; ℰ020 7565 7299; www.ltmuseum.co.uk) tells the fascinating story of the capital's public transport history with a large collection of historic vehicles, interactive displays and archive materials that really bring its subject to life.

It is well worth exploring the narrow side streets in and around Covent Garden, particularly **Neal's Yard** (off Shorts Gardens, a 2min walk from Covent Garden Underground station) complete with period hoists, dovecotes, trees in tubs, geranium-filled window boxes and a whole raft of eco-friendly shopkeepers, vegetarian and wholefood restaurants and food outlets. It's a particularly attractive spot in summer.

### The Courtauld Gallery★★
⊖Temple, Embankment, Covent Garden. Somerset House, the Strand. ⏱Open year-round daily 10am–6pm. ⏱Closed 25–26 Dec. ✍£6. Free Mon 10am–2pm (except bank hols). &✕. ℰ020 7848 2526. www.courtauld.ac.uk.

The gallery is housed in one of central London's finest riverside buildings, **Somerset House**, designed by **Sir William Chambers** and built 1776–86. Samuel Courtauld's splendid private collection of **Impressionists** is the heart of the gallery, including canvases by Manet (*Bar at the Folies-Bergère*), Degas, Bonnard, Gauguin (Tahitian scenes), Van Gogh (*Peach Trees in Blossom, Self-Portrait with Bandaged Ear*) Cézanne (*Lake at Annécy*) and Seurat. Other outstanding pieces include 30 oils by **Rubens** and six drawings by **Michelangelo** as well as works by Bruegel, Leonardo, Tiepolo, Dürer, Rembrandt, Bellini, Tintoretto and Kokoschka; paintings of the Italian Primitive school and of the Renaissance; paintings by the **Bloomsbury Group**. In the summertime Somerset House stages open-air events; in winter it is home to a spectacular ice-rink.

## SOHO★

This very cosmopolitan district (⊖ *Leicester Square, Piccadilly Circus*), where immigrants once tended to congregate, is the home of the music and film trades, and night-life of every kind. Soho is particularly popular with the gay community.

In the latter decades of the 20C it became synonymous with sex clubs, prostitution and low-life. Today, although sex clubs and sex shops can still be found, the night scene is more reputable and much safer.

The area is also famous for its concentration of good places to eat and drink, with many top French, Italian, Greek and Chinese restaurants in particular. Many of the last can be found in and around Gerrard Street, London's small **Chinatown★** district. This colourful area is marked by Oriental gates and other exotic street furniture, and abounds in eating places, supermarkets selling eastern foodstuffs and Oriental goods. At **Chinese New Year** this is the scene of one of London's most colourful street festivals.

Gerrard Street leads onto **Old Compton Street**, the spiritual heart of bohemian Soho, lined with pubs, wine merchants, pastry shops and Italian food stores. In summer grab a sandwich or snack and retreat to bucolic **Soho Square** (est. 1680), between Greek Street and Frith Street.

At **Leicester Square★** the bohemian character of Soho dissipates with the huge crowds that traverse this tree-shaded pedestrian precinct, made garish by the bright lights of many cinemas and tawdry cheap food outlets. In the run-up to the 2012 Olympics the square is being redeveloped, so you may notice lots of hoardings.

At the **TKTS Leicester Square** building (formerly known as the Half-Price Ticket Booth), regulated by the **Society of London Theatres** (⊙ *open Mon–Sat 10am–7pm for matinée and evening shows, Sun 11am–4pm, matinées only; ⊜cash only, service charge £3 per ticket, maximum four tickets per person; www. officiallondontheatre.co.uk/tkts*) you can buy tickets for leading West End shows at a significant discount, though tickets for the most popular shows are rarely, if ever available. Beware; there are other non-official reduced-price theatre ticket booths around the square who may not offer the best service.

## HOLBORN★

The medieval manors at this former crossroads have been transformed into Lincoln's Inn and Gray's Inn, two of the four Inns of Court (☾ *see below*). The fields where beasts once grazed are less in extent but still open; on the north side stands the remarkable time capsule of **Sir John Soane's Museum★★** (⊖ *Holborn; 13 Lincoln's Inn Fields; ⊙ open Tue–Sat 10am–5pm, candlelit evening first Tue of each month 6pm–9pm; arrive early, particularly on Sat and Tue evening, to avoid waiting in line; ⊙ closed bank hols, Good Fri and 24–26 Dec; ⊜free entry, £5 Tue evening; *⊶guided tour Sat 11am (⊜£5; no booking; 22 tickets on sale from 10.30am); ℘020 7405 2107; www.soane.org*). This remarkable little museum presents the highly individual collection of Classical sculpture, architectural fragments, drawings, prints and paintings, assembled by Soane, the architect, in his own house and left virtually untouched as stipulated in his will in 1833. The highlight is the **collection of pictures** mostly assembled on folding and sliding planes which make the most of the very limited available space. There are drawings by Piranesi, paintings by Canaletto, Reynolds and Turner and 12 of Hogarth's minutely observed paintings of London's unpleasant 18C underbelly including *The Election* and *The Rake's Progress*.

The area around High Holborn and Fleet Street has been the centre of legal London since the 14C, housing some of the world's oldest surviving legal training establishments: Lincoln's Inn, Gray's Inn, Inner Temple and Middle Temple, known collectively as the Four Inns of Court. Each inn (which meant house in Old English) resembles a small university campus, comprising rooms for practising barristers, a dining hall, a library and a chapel. They are oases of calm, little known to most Londoners, and the grounds and some of the buildings are open to the public from Monday to Friday. **Lincoln's Inn**★★ (⊖*Holborn; Entrances on Chancery Lane, Carey Street and Serle Street; grounds: ©open year-round Mon–Fri excl bank hols; chapel: ©open Mon–Fri (excl bank hols), noon–2.30pm; call to confirm; ℘020 7405 1393; www.lincolnsinn.org.uk*) is the grandest of the four Inns of Court, dating back to the late-15C. The Old Hall dates from 1490; the Old Buildings are Tudor, while the Chapel was rebuilt 1620–23.

The **Temple**★ (⊖*Temple; entrances on Fleet Street and Embankment; ©see website for church opening times; ⊜Temple Church £3. ℘020 7353 3470; www.temple-church.com, www.innertemple.org.uk*), another remarkable ancient complex, comprises two of the four Inns of Court, **Inner Temple** and **Middle Temple**. The gabled, half-timbered three-storey Tudor **Inner Temple Gateway** leads off Fleet Street into the Temple, past 19C buildings and the houses *(right)* where Dr Johnson (of Dictionary fame) lived in the 1760s. It leads to **Temple Church**, made famous recently by *The Da Vinci Code* movie. This was built in the 12C in the round style of the Church of the Holy Sepulchre in Jerusalem. On the stone floor lie 10 effigies of knights in armour dating from the 10C to the 13C. The highlight of Middle Temple is the magnificent **Middle Temple Hall** (©*open Mon–Fri 10–11.30am, 3–4pm (functions permitting, call ahead); ℘020 7427 4800; www.middle temple.org.uk*). The Elizabethan Great Hall has ancient oak timbers, panelling and fine carving, heraldic glass, helmets and armour and a remarkable double hammerbeam construction roof (1574). The splendid dining table is reputedly made from the hatch of Sir Francis Drake's flagship *Golden Hinde* and the suits of armour standing guard around the hall are of similar vintage.

On High Holborn **Gray's Inn**★ (⊖*Holborn; gardens: ©open Mon–Fri, noon–2.30pm; squares: ©open Mon–Fri 9am–5pm; ©both closed bank hols; www.*

*graysinn.org.uk*) was founded in the 14C. Its buildings date from the 16C though many have had to be renewed since the war. On the opposite side of the road, a contemporary survivor, from the late-16C, is the row of **half-timbered houses** (1586–96), forming the front of **Staple Inn**★, which was also once a legal training establishment, albeit never an Inn of Court.

Just around the corner is another remarkable little half-timbered house, known as the **Old Curiosity Shop** (*Portsmouth Street, SW corner of Lincoln's Inn Fields*) immortalised by Dickens in his eponymous novel (1841). It is a rare example of an Elizabethan building (c.1567) to survive intact in London. It has had many recent guises and currently sells shoes (©*open Mon–Sat 10.30am–7pm*).

## BLOOMSBURY★

This former residential area with its many squares is dominated by two learned institutions, the British Museum (*⌖see below*) and the **University of London**. The development of Bloomsbury Square in 1661 brought a new concept in social planning; the 4th Earl of Southampton erected houses for the well-to-do around three sides of the square, a mansion for himself on the fourth, northern side and a network of service streets all around. A century later, in 1775, the elegant **Bedford Square**★★ was developed. It is still complete, with its three-storey brick terrace houses with first-floor balconies. More squares, now partly incorporated into the university precinct, followed. The most famous residents were the 1920s **Bloomsbury Group** of writers, artists and philosophers, including Virginia Woolf, Vanessa Bell and Roger Fry.

### British Museum★★★

⊖*Russell Square. Great Russell Street. ©Open year-round daily 10am–5.30pm (8.30pm Fri). ©Closed Good Fri, 1 Jan, 24–26 Dec. ⊜Charge for temporary exhibitions only. ⌖Various guided tours (see website). ⌖⌖. ℘020 7323 8299. www.thebritishmuseum.ac.uk.*

Since the Millennium the British Museum has undergone the biggest revolution in its centuries-old existence. **The Great Court**, designed by Sir Norman Foster, is now the hub of the museum – its glass-and-steel roof spans the space to the Reading Room – and makes for a stunning entrance foyer.

It all began back in 1753 when Sir Hans Sloane's collection was bequeathed to the nation. This augmented the old Royal Library of 12,000 volumes assembled by monarchs since Tudor times. Acquisitions increased dramatically in the 19C and 20C with finds by archaeologists attached to the museum, bringing the museum its reputation as one of the greatest centres of world antiquities.

Notable among the Egyptian antiquities are the **mummies**, and the **Rosetta Stone**, which provided a key for deciphering heiroglyphics. No less fascinating is **Ginger** (so-named after the colour of his hair), a 5,000-year-old corpse buried in hot sands c.3300 BC and naturally preserved intact.

The collection of Western Asiatic antiquities is particularly wide-ranging, including the world-famous **Elgin Marbles** (see below). Look carefully at the exquisite Roman **Portland Vase** and you can see that it has been carefully pieced back together again after it was smashed it into 200 pieces in 1845. **Lindow Man** (1C AD), garrotted and preserved in a peat bog, is evidence of human sacrifice. Reminders of Roman Britain include the 4C silver set of tableware known as the **Mildenhall Treasure**, found in Suffolk, and considered to be the finest pieces of their kind anywhere in the Roman Empire. This was eclipsed in 1994 by the **Hoxne Hoard** – thousands of coins, jewellery and silver plate, also found in Suffolk.

In the Medieval, Renaissance and Modern Collections is the **Sutton Hoo Ship Burial**, which shows the rich variety of artefacts retrieved from a royal tomb including fabulous gold jewellery, weapons and armour. Note too the beautifully carved mid-12C walrus ivory **Lewis Chessmen** found on the Isle of Lewis in the Outer Hebrides.

The Western Asiatic section, covering Mesopotamia and Asia Minor, includes breathtaking **Assyrian sculptures** from the cities of Nimrud, Khorsabad and Nineveh. From ancient Iran the rich artistic tradition of the Persian Empire shines through in the **Luristan Bronzes** c.1200 BC, and the fabulous **Oxus Treasure** (5C–4C BC).

The circular, domed **Reading Room** (40ft/12m wide) dates from 1857, and was designed to ensure that the "poorest student" as well as men of letters should be able to have access to the library. It accommodates 400 readers and 25mi/40km of shelving (1,300,000 books). The restored blue-and-gold decoration of the dome re-creates the original setting, where Karl Marx, Lenin and George Bernard Shaw, among many others, have sat and studied

## British Library★★

Euston Square. 96 Euston Road. *Galleries:* Open Mon–Sat, 9.30am–6pm (Tue 8pm, Sat 5pm), Sun and bank hols 11am–5pm. ♿ ✗.
℘0843 208 1144. www.bl.uk.

The British Library houses the world's second-largest collection of written works after the Library of Congress in the USA. Opened in 1997, the St Pancras building (there are other branches) is a monumental free-form, asymmetric structure of red brick, Welsh slate and metal and granite. The entrance piazza is dominated by a huge bronze statue of Newton by Sir Eduardo Paolozzi.

The library's most famous treasures, on display in the **Sir John Ritblat Gallery**, include a copy of **Magna Carta**, the **Lindisfarne Gospel**, **Codex Sinaiticus**, the Gutenberg Bible, the Diamond Sutra, Nelson's last letter, Shakespeare's signature and **First Folio** (1623), and Beatles' manuscripts. Advanced technology makes it possible to turn the pages of rare books (if only virtually) at the touch of a button. There are two other permanent galleries, devoted to philately and conservation, as well as temporary exhibitions.

## REGENT'S PARK★★

This beautiful park (⊖Regent's Park), bounded to the north by the Regent's Canal, and surrounded by dazzling white Regency terraces and splendid villas, was laid out in the early-19C by John Nash. The park has long been famous for its zoo, and is much loved for its rose garden and boating lake. Bordering it to the south is the busy Marylebone Road and Madame Tussaud's.

### London Zoo (ZSL)★★

⊖Regent's Park, Camden Town. Outer Circle, Regent's Park. ⏰Open daily 10am–5.30pm/6pm (4pm Nov–Feb); last entry 1hr before closing. Also open Jun–Jul Fri 6–10pm. ⏰Closed 25 Dec. ☞£17.60–£18.60, child £13.70–£14.50. Book online to avoid queues ⟨⟩✕. ☎0844 225 1826. www. londonzoo.co.uk.

The Zoological Society of London (ZSL) opened on a 5-acre/2ha site in Regent's Park in 1828. Today it covers 36 acres/14ha with around 8,000 animals from 900 species. The emphasis nowadays is placed on breeding endangered animals and on foreign conservation projects.

The zoo's once-famous elephants have been transferred to an outreach (Whipsnade Park, where they have more space) but there are still family favourites such as lions, tigers, rhinos and giraffes to see. Pick up a programme of activities and plan your visit around that.

### Madame Tussaud's★ (C1)

⊖Baker Street. ⏰Open daily year-round 9am/9.30am–5.30pm/7pm (last entry), see website for details. ⏰Closed 25 Dec. ☞£28.80. £14.40 after 5pm/6pm. (book online to avoid queues and for 10 percent discount). ⟨⟩. ☎0871 894 3000. www.madame-tussauds.com.

The famous waxworks include Louis XV's mistress, portrayed as Sleeping Beauty, made by Madame Tussaud herself, plus statesmen of several ages and countries, modern celebrities in the worlds of sport and entertainment, murderers at the scene of their crimes in the Chamber of Horrors (complete with live actors) as well as a ride through the history of London.

# City of London★★★

## SIGHTS
### St Paul's Cathedral★★★

⊖St Paul's. ⏰Open Mon–Sat 8.30am–4pm (last entry). Galleries 9.30am–4.15pm. Sun services only (entry free). ☞£14.50 (£12.50 online ☞Guided tours free. ⟨⟩✕. ☎020 7236 4128; 0207 246 8350 (recorded info). www.stpauls.co.uk.

The present cathedral, the fourth or fifth on a site dating back to AD 604, is the masterpiece of **Sir Christopher Wren** (1632–1723). After the Great Fire of 1666, Old St Paul's was a ruin. The foundation stone of the new cathedral was laid on 21 June 1675 and 33 years later Wren saw his son set the final stone in place – the topmost in the lantern. When Wren died 15 years later he was buried within the walls. Beneath the dome his own epitaph reads in Latin: "Reader, if you seek his monument, look around you."

**Exterior** – The most striking feature is the **dome**, even today a dominant feature of the City skyline. Unlike the dome of St Peter's, which influenced Wren, it is not a true hemisphere. The drum below it is in two tiers, the lower encircled by columns and crowned by a balustrade, the upper recessed behind the balustrade so as to afford a circular viewing gallery, the **Stone Gallery**. On top of the dome, the lantern features columns on all four sides and a small cupola serving as a plinth to the 6.5ft-/2m-diameter golden ball.

The **west end**, approached by two wide flights of steps, is composed of a two-tier portico of columns below a decorated pediment surmounted by St Paul. On either side rise Wren's Baroque spires. A notable feature of the exterior is the

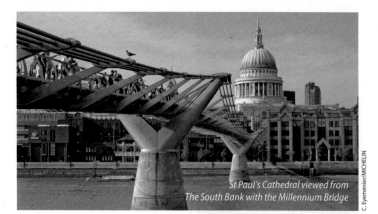

*St Paul's Cathedral viewed from The South Bank with the Millennium Bridge*

C. Eyemenier/MICHELIN

profuse carving by **Grinling Gibbons** and others.

**Interior** – The impression is one of space, of almost luminescent stone and, in the distance, gold and mosaic.

A 270-degree film exhibition, ***Oculus; An Eye into St Paul's*** traces both the cathedral's 1,400 year-history and its daily life. "Virtual access" films also cover the dome and galleries.

In the **nave** the entire space between two piers in the north aisle is occupied by the Wellington monument; in the south aisle hangs Holman Hunt's *The Light of the World*. From the **Whispering Gallery** in the dome *(259 steps)* there are impressive views of the concourse below, and close views of the interior of the dome, painted by Thornhill. A whisper spoken close to the wall can be clearly heard on the diametrically opposite side. The **views**★★★ from the **Golden Gallery** at the top of the dome are better than from the Stone Gallery *(543 steps)*. In the **choir** the dark oak stalls are the exquisite work of Grinling Gibbons. The iron railing, the gates to the choir aisles and the great gilded screens enclosing the sanctuary are the work of Jean Tijou. The graceful sculpture of the Virgin and Child in the north aisle is by Henry Moore (1984). In the south aisle is a rare pre-Fire relic, a scorch-marked statue of **John Donne**, the great poet and Dean of St Paul's 1621–31. The **Crypt** contains tombs of many illustrious individuals and memorials, too numerous to list.

## Barbican★

The Barbican complex (built 1962–82) combines residential accommodation with schools, shops, open spaces, a conference and arts centre, a medieval church and the Museum of London.

### Museum of London★★

⊖*Barbican, Moorgate. London Wall.* ⏱*Open year-round daily 10am–6pm.* ⏱*Closed 24–26 Dec.* ♿✖. ℘*020 7001 9844. www.museumoflondon.org.uk.* The biggest city history museum in the world presents the story of London from prehistory to the present day, with exhibits as various as the sculptures from the Roman temple of Mithras, medieval pilgrim badges, the Cheapside Hoard of Jacobean jewellery, a diorama of the Great Fire, the doors from Newgate Gaol, 19C shops and interiors, the Lord Mayor's Coach, souvenirs of the women's suffrage movement… right through the swinging 60s and into 21C issues.

### ♟♟ Tower of London★★★

⊖*Tower Hill.* ⏱*Open Mar–Oct Tue–Sat 9am–5.30pm, Sun–Mon 10am–5.30pm. Nov–Feb closes 4.30pm.* ⏱*Closed 1 Jan, 24–26 Dec.* ⊜*£18, child £9.50. Buy tickets online (at a discount) or by phone (℘0844 482 7777; £2 service charge) to save waiting time.* ☞ *Guided tour (1hr) by Yeoman Warders. Last tour: summer 3.30pm, winter 2.30pm. Free.* ♿✖. ℘*0844 482 7777. www.hrp.org.uk.*

*White Tower, Tower of London*

VisitLondonImages/britainonview/Pawel Libera

In 1067 William I constructed a wooden fortress then replaced it with one in stone (c.1077–97) in order to deter Londoners from revolt; its river site also gave immediate sighting of any hostile force coming up the Thames. Norman, Plantagenet and Tudor successors recognised its value and extended it until it occupied 18 acres/7ha.

From 1300 to 1810 the Tower housed the Royal Mint; because of its defences it became the Royal Jewel House and also served as a feared prison. Monarchs have been associated with the Tower from William the Conqueror to Elizabeth I.

The **Jewel House** (*queues tend to be shorter early in the day*) displays the **Crown Jewels**★★★ which date from the Restoration to the present day, almost all of the earlier regalia having been sold or melted down by Oliver Cromwell. The **Chapel of St Peter ad Vincula**, consecrated in the 12C, rebuilt in the 13C and 16C, is the burial place of several dukes and two of Henry VIII's queens, beheaded in the Tower.

**Traitors' Gate** was the main entrance to the Tower when the Thames was still London's principal thoroughfare; later, when the river served only for secret access, the entrance acquired its chilling name. The Bloody Tower gained its name in the 16C and was perhaps the place where the "Princes in the Tower"

were murdered in 1483. Sir Walter Raleigh was imprisoned here 1603–1615. The **White Tower**★★★ keep is one of the earliest fortifications on such a scale in western Europe, begun by William I in 1078 and completed 20 years later by William Rufus. The 100ft-/30m-high stone walls form an uneven quadrilateral, its corners marked by one circular and three square towers. The **Armour Collection**, one of the world's greatest, was started by Henry VIII and increased under Charles II. On the second floor, **St John's Chapel**★★ remains much as it was when completed in 1080, a 55ft-/17m-long stone chapel rising through two floors. An inner line of great round columns with simply carved capitals bears circular Norman arches and is echoed above in a second tier.

**Beauchamp Tower**★, built in the 13C, has served as a prison since the 14C. The walls of the main chamber are inscribed with prisoners' graffiti.

## Tower Bridge★★

⊖ Tower Hill, London Bridge. Riverboat to Tower Pier. Tower Bridge Road. *Open daily, Apr–Sept 10am–6.30pm. Oct–Mar 9.30am–6pm. Closed 24–26 Dec. £8. 020 7403 3761. www.towerbridge.org.uk.*

The familiar Gothic towers, high-level walkways and the original engine rooms form part of the tour which traces the design of the bridge by Sir John Wolfe-Barry and Horace Jones, its construction (1886–94) and explains the functioning of the hydraulic mechanism which, until 1976, raised the 1,100ton drawbridge-like bascules (now driven by electricity).

## St Katharine Docks★

In 1828 **Thomas Telford** developed this series of basins and warehouses next to The City and they prospered for over a hundred years. After wartime bombing, however, the dock was abandoned until 1968, when moorings were organised for private yachts. Telford's main Italianate-style building was restored as **Ivory House** with apartments above a shopping arcade. Restaurants and bars now proliferate the dock.

# Southwark★

In the 16C the borough of Southwark was infamous for its brothels and theatres, on account of its location outside the jurisdiction of the City of London. Near the site of the original Globe Theatre, where Shakespeare's plays were performed, now stands the landmark **Shakespeare's Globe**★★ which replicates the original 16C structure. The Elizabethan playhouse's stage thrusts into a large circular yard surrounded by three tiers of roofed seating in the round. **Stage productions**★★ are held in this authentic outdoor setting each summer (*late Apr– early Oct, see website, below, for schedule*) and the site also has an excellent permanent **exhibition**★ (⊖*Mansion House, London Bridge; 21 New Globe Walk;* ⏰*open daily winter 10am–5pm, in summer when matinées play, no access to Globe Theatre, tour of Exhibition and Rose Theatre 9–12.30pm (11.30am Sun) or 1am–5pm (Sun noon–5pm);* ⏰*closed 24–25 Dec;* ⌨*£9/11.50;* ♿✗; ✆*020 7902 1400; www.shakespearesglobe.com*).

The most spectacular local medieval building is the **George Inn**★, still a functioning pub, built round three sides of a courtyard, although only one of the galleried ranges has survived.

Along the river old warehouses have been converted to new uses – **Hays Galleria** with its shops, pubs and modern sculpture, and the acclaimed **Design Museum** (⊖*Tower Hill; Shad Thames;* ⏰*open year-round daily 10am–5.45pm;* ⏰*closed 25–26 Dec;* ⌨*£10;* ♿✗; ✆*020 7403 6933; www.designmuseum.org*), are two examples. The latter illustrates the evolution of contemporary design.

## LONDON BRIDGE

These days London Bridge is (in-)famous for two horror-themed visitor attractions. The long-established **London Dungeon**★ (👥; ⊖*London Bridge; Tooley Street;* ⏰*open year-round daily; summer and holidays 9.30am–6.30pm; other times of year 10am/10.30am–5pm/5.30pm;* ⏰*closed 25 Dec;* ⌨*£23.10, child £17.10; buy timed tickets in advance to make significant savings and to avoid waiting time;* ♿✗; ✆*020 7403 7221.; www.thedungeons.com*) under the station arches is a gruesome all-too-lifelike exhibition of death, disease, disaster and torture in past centuries. It also features theme-park-style rides and is hugely popular with gore-loving teens but is wholly unsuitable for young children.

Almost adjacent, also under London Bridge, is the relatively new **London Bridge Experience** (👥; ⊖*London Bridge. Tooley Street;* ⏰*open year-round Mon–Fri 10am–5pm (last entry), Sat–Sun 10am–6pm (last entry); 24 Dec–1 Jan 1am–4pm (last entry);* ⏰*closed 25 Dec;* ⌨*£23, child £17; buy timed tickets in advance to make significant savings and to avoid waiting time;* ♿✗; ✆*0800 0434 666; www.thelondonbridgeexperience.com*), that weaves ghostly happenings and special effects into the colourful history of London Bridge. It has genuine historical interest and humour, but also features a good dose of terror and is not suitable for young children.

Also on Tooley Street (nos. 64–66) is **Winston Churchill's Britain at War Experience**★ (⊖*London Bridge;* ⏰*open year-round daily 10am–5pm (4.30pm Nov–Mar);* ⏰*closed 24–26 Dec;* ⌨*£12.95;* ♿; ✆*020 7403 3171; www.britainatwar.co.uk*), a re-creation of the London Blitz of the 1940s in all its fury with special effects of sights and sounds,

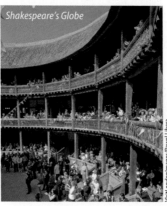

Shakespeare's Globe

VisitLondonImages/Pawel Libera

## Blue Plaques

All over the capital you will find blue plaques affixed to buildings where famous people have lived. In total there are over 760 in London including actors, authors, politicians, painters, scientists, sportsmen, campaigners and reformers – people from different countries, cultures and backgrounds have all been commemorated in this way. In order to be eligible for a plaque there are a number of criteria to be met: the person must have been dead for 20 years, or have passed the centenary of their birth, whichever is the earlier; be considered eminent by a majority of members of their own profession or calling; have made an important positive contribution to human welfare or happiness; be recognisable to the well-informed passer-by; deserve national recognition; have resided in a locality for a significant period, in time or importance, within their life and work. To illustrate their diversity, in Mayfair there is a plaque to George Frideric Handel at 25 Brook Street and next door at no. 23 a plaque to Jimi Hendrix.

artefacts, and even the dust and smoke of an air raid.

Head to the river from here and you will find **HMS Belfast** (⊖ *London Bridge; Morgan's Lane, Tooley Street;* 🕐*open daily 10am–6pm (5pm Nov–Feb);* 🕐*closed 24–26 Dec;* ﷼*£12.25;* ✕*;* ☎*020 7940 6300; http://hmsbelfast.iwm.org.uk).* This great grey cruiser (1938) moored against the south bank of the Thames saw service with the North Atlantic Convoys and on D-Day in 1944.

Follow the riverbank west and you will come to **Southwark Cathedral**★★ (⊖ *London Bridge;* 🕐*open year-round daily 8am–6pm (Sat–Sun and bank hols 8.30am–6pm);* ﷼*£4 contribution requested;* ♿✕*;* ☎*020 7367 700; http:// cathedral.southwark.anglican.org/)* on the other side of London Bridge. The cathedral began life in 1106 and its earliest work is the fragment of a Norman arch in the north wall. The massive piers supporting the central tower and the Early English **chancel** date from the 13C. The **altar screen** (1520) appears in sumptuous Gothic glory; it remained empty until 1905 when statues were carved to fill the niches. The nave was rebuilt in 1890–97 to harmonise with the chancel. Notable features are the **Harvard Chapel**, the 1616 **monument** to Alderman Humble and his wives, and the 12 **bosses** rescued from the 15C wooden roof which collapsed in 1830. The cathedral bounds **Borough Market**★

(⊖ *London Bridge; Borough High Street;* 🕐*open year-round Thu 11am–5pm, Fri noon–6pm, Sat 8am–5pm;* ♿*;* ☎*020 7407 1002; www.boroughmarket. org.uk),* not only London's oldest food market but also the country's most important retail market for fine foods. Food lovers of every kind, from curious tourists and hungry students, to celebrity London chefs, come here to shop or merely drool over the mouthwatering range of delights. There are several stalls offering ready-to-eat food either to take away or to eat in, at small tables next to the market stall.

Continuing west from here along the river you come to the **Golden Hinde** (👥*;* ⊖ *London Bridge, Monument. St Mary Overie Dock;* 🕐*open Mon–Sat 10am–5.30pm (check website for private events);* ﷼*£6, child £4.50;* ☎*020 7403 0123; http://goldenhinde.com).* "Hands-on" learning with costumed interpreters is the order of the day on board this full-size seaworthy replica of Sir Francis Drake's 16C flagship, in which he circumnavigated the world.

## SOUTH BANK AND LAMBETH

Head west along the river from London Bridge to the landmark **Tate Modern**★★ (⊖ *Southwark, Blackfriars. Bankside;* 🕐*open year-round daily 10am (galleries 10.15am)–6pm (Fri–Sat 10pm);* 🕐*closed 24–26 Dec;* ﷼*charge only for temporary exhibitions;* ♿🅿*(disabled visitors only)* ✕*;* ☎*020 7887 8888; www.tate.org.uk).*

The former Bankside Power Station, with its single chimney (325ft/99m) and giant internal dimensions, makes a striking home for this major gallery, devoted to international 20C and 21C art. The wealth of the collection is largely due to the bequests of Sir Roland Penrose, one-time friend of Picasso and Ernst, and that of Edward James, a former patron to Dalí and Magritte. Gigantic sculptures by contemporary artists are set off by the vast spaces of the Turbine Hall (500ft/152m long and 115ft/35m high), where overhead cranes recall the building's working life. Themed displays mean that you can never quite be sure what will be here at any one time. World-class special exhibitions are regularly staged.

Further west is the **Southbank Centre**★★ (⊖ Waterloo; www.southbankcentre. co.uk, www.nationaltheatre.org.uk, www. bfi.org.uk), the UK's most important arts and theatre complex. The Brutalist-style grey concrete buildings house: the **National Theatre**, which stages the finest theatre productions in the country outside London's West End; the **BFI (British Film Institute) Southbank**, formerly known as the National Film Theatre, which screens both classic and cult movies; the **Royal Festival Hall** specialises in orchestral concerts; the **Queen Elizabeth Hall** hosts chamber orchestras, quartets, choirs, dance performances and opera (and also contains the Purcell Room); the **Hayward Gallery** has a rotating exhibition of contemporary art.

Bookshops, cafés, restaurants and live foyer events ensure that the South Bank is lively for much of the day as well as during evening performances.

Carrying on west along the riverbank you will find the **London Eye**★★ (**E3**;⊖Westminster; South Bank; ticket office in County Hall. Ⓞopen daily year-round, from 10am. Sept–Dec closes 8.30pm, for rest of year see website; due to its huge popularity, visitors should book a time slot in advance; a limited number of tickets are sold on-site every day; Ⓞclosed 25 Dec and second week Jan for annual maintenance; from £18.60 (10 percent discount online); &.✖; ✆0800 093 0123 (enquiries); 0871 781 3000 (bookings); www.londoneye.com). On the opposite side of the river to Parliament this giant observation wheel is a spectacular Millennium landmark on the Thames. Sightseers are accommodated in glass pods to enjoy unparalleled **views**★★★ of London 443ft/135m high during their 30-minute ride.

Next to the Eye, inside County Hall are two attractions. The **London Sea Life Aquarium**★ (**E3**; ▲▲; ⊖Westminster. County Hall; Ⓞopen year-round daily 10am–6pm (Sat–Sun 7pm); £19.02, child £14.04 (significant discounts online); &.✖; 0871 663 1678; www.londonaquarium.co.uk) is one of Europe's largest aquariums with sharks in spectacular large-scale tanks, piranhas at feeding time and stingrays in a touch-tank. There are also exhibits on local and British marine life. The **London Film Museum** (**E3**; ⊖Westminster; County Hall; Ⓞopen year-round daily 10am/11am–5pm/6pm; £13.50;&; ✆020 7202 7040; www.the moviuem.com) opened in 2008, concentrates mostly on British films, but also has enough of international interest for most regular cinema fans.

A short walk away, the other side of Westminster Bridge, is the **Imperial War Museum**★★★ (**F3**; ⊖Lambeth North, Elephant and Castle; Lambeth Road; Ⓞopen year-round daily 10am–6pm; charge for temporary exhibitions; &.✖; ✆020 7416 5000; www.iwm. org.uk). One of the world's finest war museums, this sensitive and thought-provoking exhibition honours both civilians and those who have served during wartime.

A wide range of weapons and equipment is on display: armoured fighting vehicles, field guns and small arms, together with models, decorations, uniforms, posters and photographs, masses of archive material, including moving first-hand oral accounts of warfare, as well as a selection from the museum's outstanding collection based on the work of two generations of official war artists.

# Inner Suburbs★★

## CAMDEN

Set immediately north of Regent's Park, gritty **Camden** (⊖Camden Town) provides a stark contrast to the park's grand Palladian villas. This is one of London's more bohemian areas and is famous for its **markets**★★ (Camden Market, Camden Lock Market and Canal Market), which sell antiques, fashion and bric-a-brac, catering to a young and alternative lifestyle. The area is also lively by night with good **live music** venues, down-to-earth pubs and cheap eats.

## KNIGHTSBRIDGE

One of London's most exclusive suburbs, Knightsbridge (⊖Knightsbridge) is synonymous with **Harrods**★★ (est 1849), the world's most famous department store, and its neighbour, **Harvey Nichols**★, where "ladies who lunch" come for the very best in fashion, beauty and home accessories. Both stores are renowned for their displays; "Harvey Nicks" for its window dressing and Harrods for its cornucopian turn-of-the-century **Food Halls**. At night, Harrods' famous terra-cotta façade, added in 1901, is illuminated by around 11,000 lightbulbs and is a fine sight.

## KENSINGTON★★

Kensington is one of London's wealthiest suburbs. South Kensington is home to three world-famous national museums (⌖see below). **Kensington High Street** (⊖) offers local as well as brand-name shops and just off here, **Holland Park** (⊖) is a pretty, bucolic retreat from the crowds. Immediately north is **Notting Hill** (⊖), famous for its huge Rio-style **carnival** (last weekend Aug), and weekly (Sat) **Portobello Road Market**.

The antiques market here is claimed to be the world's largest; many of the shops are also open in the week.

### Kensington Palace★★ (BY)

⊖Queensway, High Street Kensington. ⊙Open daily 10am–6pm (Nov–Feb 5pm). ⊙Closed 24–26 Dec. ⊚£12.50. ⌖. ℘0844 482 7799. www.hrp.org.uk.

This early-17C Jacobean house has passed through three principal phases: under the House of Orange it was William III's private residence, with **Sir Christopher Wren** as principal architect; under the early Hanoverians it became a royal palace, with William Kent in charge of decorative schemes; since 1760 it has been a residence for members of the royal family, most notably the late **Diana, Princess of Wales**. The **State Apartments** are approached by the Queen's Staircase, designed by Wren. The **Queen's Gallery** has carving by Grinling Gibbons and portraits by Kneller and Lely. The **Privy** and lofty **Presence Chamber, Cupola** and **Drawing Rooms**, added for George I in 1718–20, were decorated by William Kent during 1722–27, covering the walls and ceiling with trompe l'œil paintings.

For many visitors the highlight is the **Royal Ceremonial Dress Collection** of 12,000 items worn by royalty and courtiers from the 17C to the present day, including clothing worn by George III, Queen Victoria, Princess Margaret, the Queen, and Diana, Princess of Wales.

The palace reopens to visitors in late March 2012 following major renovations which promise to make for a much richer and less formal visit than in the past.

### Kensington Gardens★★ (B2/3)

⊖Queensway, High Street Kensington. At weekends the gardens are a favourite walk with Kensington locals, most famously nannies with their small charges. The **Round Pond** is the focal point for avenues radiating northeast, east and southeast to the **Serpentine**, where rowing boats may be hired, and **Long Water**. The early-18C **Orangery**★, Hawksmoor's splendid Baroque centrepiece (1705), now houses a restaurant. Beyond the Flower Walk on the south side of the gardens stands the **Albert Memorial**★ (1876), designed by George Gilbert Scott. Beneath a highly ornamented Gothic Revival spire surrounded by statues and a frieze of 169 named figures of poets, artists, architects and composer, sits a bronze statue (14ft/4.2m) of the Prince Consort who did so much to further the arts and learning, until his premature death in 1861.

Opposite stands the **Royal Albert Hall**★ (1867–71), a popular venue for meetings, conferences and concerts, notably the eight-week summer season of **Promenade Concerts**.

## Hyde Park★★ (C2/3)

Adjoining Kensington Gardens to the east, Hyde Park (⊖*Marble Arch, High Street Kensington, Hyde Park Corner)* is less formally laid out and very popular with office-workers and tourists alike, who come to enjoy the fresh air.

**Speakers' Corner (CX)** is a relatively modern feature of the park; not until 1872 did the government recognise the need for a place of public assembly and free discussion. Anyone can stand up and speak here as they frequently do on a Sunday morning, as long as they are not blasphemous, nor must they incite a breach of the peace. To its north stands **Marble Arch (CX)**, the triumphal arch designed by John Nash in 1827 as a grand entrance to Buckingham Palace in commemoration of the battles of Trafalgar and Waterloo. Embarrassingly it was never used, as it was too narrow to accommodate the royal Gold Stage Coach, and eventually ended up here.

## ☖☖ Natural History Museum★★★ (B3)

⊖*South Kensington. Cromwell Road.* ⏰*Open year-round daily 10am–5.50pm.* ⏰*Closed 24–26 Dec.* ✆*Charge for special exhibitions.* ♿✖. ➳*Tours.* ✆*020 7942 5000. www.nhm.ac.uk.*

Alfred Waterhouse's vast palace, inspired by medieval Rhineland architecture, was opened in 1881 to house the British Museum's ever-growing natural history collection, which today illustrates all forms of life, from the smallest bacteria to the largest creatures. This is now one of the country's favourite family museums, superbly combining education and entertainment with spectacular exhibits such as the famous **blue whale** model and huge **dinosaur skeletons**. Dinosaurs and fossils are still most visitors' favourite area and the diplodocus skeleton in the foyer has become a museum icon. Elsewhere you can learn about human biology, creepy crawlies, the origin of the species, take a behind-the-scenes tour, visit the Earth Galleries and get caught in a real earthquake simulation. The latest major development is the fascinating **Darwin Centre**, dedicated to evolution.

## ☖☖ Science Museum★★★ (B3)

⊖*South Kensington. Exhibition Road.* ⏰*Open daily 10am–6pm (7pm during school hols).* ⏰*Closed 24–26 Dec.* ✆*Free except IMAX cinema, simulators and special exhibitions.* ♿✖. ✆*0870 870 4868. www.sciencemuseum.org.uk.*

This world-beating factory-laboratory of Man's continuing invention extends over 7 acres/3ha. Large-scale exhibits range from early beam engines to actual spacecraft, the first biplanes to jet aircraft, historic railway engines, road vehicles, and it is quite easy to spend a whole day here simply marvelling at the hardware without the need for any technical knowledge.

For more enquiring minds there are innumerable working models, handles to pull, buttons to push, huge floor areas devoted completely to **hands-on** experiments and cutting-edge technology. Children (and adults) also love the **IMAX** theatre with its 3-D films. Try not to miss the often-overlooked **Wellcome Galleries** or the **History of Medicine**, on the upper floors.

## Victoria and Albert Museum★★★ (C3)

⊖*South Kensington. Entrances in Cromwell Road and Exhibition Road.* ⏰*Open year-round daily 10am–5.45pm (selected galleries 10pm Fri).* ⏰*Closed 24 Dec–26.* ✆*Charge for special exhibitions.* ➳*Guided tours.* ♿✖. ✆*020 7942 2000. www.vam.ac.uk.*

This fabulously rich and varied collection was started, in part, with the purchase of contemporary works manufactured for the Great Exhibition of 1851. It includes the national collection of furniture, British sculpture, textiles, ceramics, silver and watercolours, as well as world-famous displays of fashionable dress, jewellery, Italian Renaissance sculpture, and art from India and the Far East. Even by London museum standards this is a huge rambling collection and for newcomers its size is overwhelming.

**Renaissance sculptures** – The most highly prized work is Michelangelo's *Slave*, a wax model for a figure intended for the tomb of Pope Julius II.

**Cast courts** – Plaster casts made 1860–1880 for art students who could not go abroad to see the real thing, include Trajan's Column, *St George* (Donatello) and *Dying Slave* (Michelangelo).

**Prints**, **drawings and paintings** – The most valuable collection here is the **Raphael Cartoons**, seven huge tapestry patterns, commissioned in 1515 by Pope Leo X for the Sistine Chapel.

**Furniture and woodwork** – The collection ranges from the Middle Ages to the present day and encompasses just about every culture. **The Great Bed of Ware**, mentioned by Shakespeare, is the most remarkable piece of ancient British furniture. It is said to have once slept 52 people (26 butchers and their wives).

**Textiles and dress** – ne of the world's most extensive collections of textiles.

**Metalworks and jewellery** – This is perhaps the most diverse and eclectic national collection, ranging from the 2C BC to the 21C AD, and encompasses a very broad spectrum and some magnificent pieces. The **Gilbert Collection** of gold, silver, micro-mosaics and gold boxes is a beautiful recent addition.

**Eastern works of art** – Some 60,000 artefacts from China, Korea and Japan. The most famous exhibit is **Tipu's Tiger**, a near-lifes-size painted wooden tiger mauling its white victim. Within the tiger is an organ that simulates both the tiger's roars and its victim's groans.

## CHELSEA★★

Riverside Chelsea (⊖*Sloane Square, Pimlico*) has always attracted artists, architects, writers and actors. Chelsea once had a reputation for fashionable bohemian living, but it is currently better known as a well-heeled suburb. In 1955 the opening of Bazaar clothes boutique by Mary Quant led to a radical change in dress with the launch of the mini skirt. During the 1960s, the **King's Road**★ became "the navel of swinging London", then in 1971, Chelsea fashion was re-invigorated by Vivienne Westwood, who opened her clothes shop at 430 Kings Road. The road became the launching point for the Punk movement. Punk fashions are rarely seen here today, but you may spot the occasional celebrity.

### Royal Hospital★ (CD4)

*Royal Hospital Road.* **Hospital:** ⏲*Open daily, 10am–noon and 2–4pm, closed Sun during Oct–Mar and bank hols.* **Grounds:** ⏲*Open daily 10am (Sun 2pm)–dusk.* ✆*020 7881 5200. www.chelsea-pensioners.co.uk.*

The Royal Hospital was founded by King Charles II in 1682 as a retreat for veterans of the regular army who had been retired from duty after 20 years' service, or had become unfit for duty, as a result of wounds or disease. Wren produced a quadrangular plan and today the hospital still fulfils its original purpose; the **Chapel**, **Great Hall** and **Museum** *(museum Mon–Fri only)* are open to visitors. Every summer, the **Chelsea Flower Show** is held in the hospital grounds, attracting thousands of visitors.

## PIMLICO

### Tate Britain★★★ (E4)

⊖*Pimlico, then 5min walk (signed). Millbank.* ⏲*Open year-round daily, 10am–6pm (first Fri of month 10pm).* ⏲*Closed 24–26 Dec.* ⊜*Charge for temporary exhibitions only.* ⏷ *Guided tours Mon–Fri hourly 11am–3pm, Sat–Sun noon, 3pm.* ♿✗. ✆*020 7887 8888. www.tate.org.uk.*

In 1897 Henry Tate, sugar broker and British art collector, offered his collection to the nation and £80,000 for a building, if the government would provide a site. The museum is devoted exclusively to British art from 1500 to the present day. The **Clore Gallery Turner Collection** is a highlight and is one of the relatively few permanent exhibits.

# Outer London★★

### GREENWICH★★★
## London's Maritime Centre

The Tudors preferred Greenwich to their other royal residences and Henry VIII, who was born here, built a vast palace with a royal armoury; he also founded naval dockyards at neighbouring Deptford and Woolwich. During the Commonwealth, however, the palace became derelict and only the Queen's House survived (☾see below).

After the Restoration, Charles II commissioned John Webb, a student of Inigo Jones, to build a King's House. William and Mary, who preferred Hampton Court (☾see below), granted a charter for the foundation of a Royal Hospital for Seamen at Greenwich, with **Wren** as surveyor. In 1873 the Webb and Wren buildings were transformed into the Royal Naval College, and eventually the Queen's House became part of the National Maritime Museum.

### National Maritime Museum★★

*Romney Road. ◷Open year-round daily 10am–5pm (Royal Observatory/ Meridian Courtyard 6.30pm summer weekends, bank hols and school hols). Timed ticket to planetarium shows. ⊚£6.50 planetarium, £10 Royal Observatory/Meridian Courtyard. ⅷ✕. ☎020 8858 4422; 020 8312 6565. www.nmm.ac.uk.* As part of its £20 million Millennium makeover this museum of Britain's naval past – the largest maritime collection in the world with over two million seafaring-related objects – boasts an impressive single-span glazed roof, the largest in Europe, above a Neoclassical courtyard. The museum's new centrepiece gallery, opened 2011, is the **Sammy Ofer** wing, home to **Voyagers**, telling the story of Britain and the sea, illustrating the contemporary significance of maritime histories. For children, the **Bridge** links with the **All Hands** interactive gallery. Within the complex is the **Queen's House**★★. This elegant white Palladian villa was commissioned by James I from Inigo Jones, who designed it in 1615 as the very first Classical mansion.

### Millennium Dome to O2

Built to celebrate the Millennium and sited right on the Meridian Line, the Millennium Dome is the largest single-roofed structure in the world. Its external appearance is that of a huge (1,197ft/365m diameter) white marquee held up by twelve 312ft-/95m-high towers. Its circumference exceeds 0.62mi/1km and the floor space is large enough to park 18,000 London buses. Now known as the O2, it stages major concerts and other events (*www.theo2.co.uk*).

National Maritime Museum, Queens House, Old Royal Naval Collage and Canary Wharf viewed from Greenwich Park

© Jon Arnold/hemis.fr

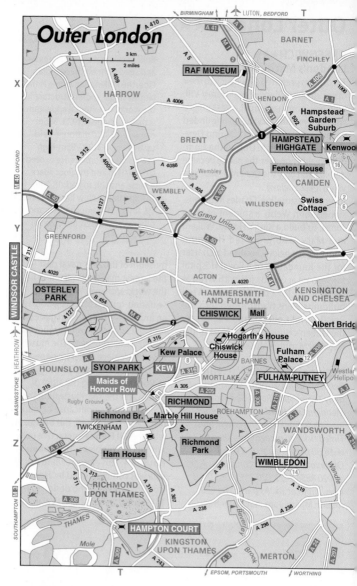

## Outer London

BIRMINGHAM — LUTON, BEDFORD — T

BARNET

FINCHLEY

RAF MUSEUM

HARROW

HENDON

Hampstead Garden Suburb

HAMPSTEAD HIGHGATE

Kenwoo

BRENT

Fenton House

CAMDEN

Wembley

WEMBLEY

WILLESDEN

Swiss Cottage

Grand Union Canal

GREENFORD

EALING

ACTON

KENSINGTON AND CHELSEA

OSTERLEY PARK

HAMMERSMITH AND FULHAM

Albert Bridg

CHISWICK — Mall

Hogarth's House

Chiswick House

Fulham Palace

Kew Palace

HOUNSLOW

SYON PARK — KEW

BARNES

Westla Helipo

Maids of Honour Row

MORTLAKE

FULHAM-PUTNEY

Rugby Ground

RICHMOND

ROEHAMPTON

Richmond Br. — Marble Hill House

TWICKENHAM

WANDSWORTH

Ham House

Richmond Park

WIMBLEDON

RICHMOND UPON THAMES

THAMES

HAMPTON COURT

Mole

KINGSTON UPON THAMES

MERTON

T — EPSOM, PORTSMOUTH — WORTHING

WINDSOR CASTLE

BASINGSTOKE HEATHROW

SOUTHAMPTON

OXFORD

**Greenwich Park and Royal Observatory**★ – The park, the oldest enclosed royal domain, extends for 180 acres /73ha, rising to a point 155ft/47m above the river, crowned by the Old Royal Observatory, built by Wren in 1675 "for finding out the longitude of places for perfect navigation and astronomy" (*entry free, included with National Maritime Museum ticket;* ), and the **General Wolfe** Monument.

Inside Wren's brick **Flamsteed House** is the lofty Octagon Room, beautifully proportioned, equipped with what John Evelyn called "the choicest instrument". The **Meridian Building** was added in the mid-18C to house the growing **telescope collection**★★. Note Airey's Transit Circle, through which the meridian passes, and outside, in the Meridian Courtyard, a brass rail marking the meridian of 0°, which visitors enjoy